D0943996

ANNUAL 1974

contents

Illustrations by J. A. Berriman,
E. A. Hodges, S. J. Aspey

Edited by Mae Broadley.

Copyright © MCMLXXIII by
World Distributors (Manchester) Limited

All rights reserved throughout the world

Published in Great Britain by
World Distributors (Manchester) Limited
P.O. Box 111, 12 Lever Street
Manchester M60 1TS

Printed in the Netherlands

SBN 7235 0189 0

A SORT OF FANFARE

by Angela R. Griffiths
A battle in one-up-manship

"Well, I can't stand her! What do you make of her?" I said to Jane as I stretched out on the classroom window ledge. The soft warmth of the sun made me wish that the lunch break would last more than one measly hour.

Jane was leaning back in her chair and her feet, minus shoes, were up on her desk. She had a mouthful of crisps but that did not prevent her making big-eyed grimaces. "The new girl, you mean?" She screwed up the empty crisp bag and aimed it at the wastepaper basket. "Proper little Madam, in my opinion. Needs taking down a peg."

I knew that Jane would agree with me. We think alike on things that really matter. And the new girl had made a bad impression, right from the start. Stuck up, snobby, know-it-all, show-off; how else could you describe the one and only Amanda Pitkin-Smythe?

But don't misjudge us. We are not usually lacking in benevolence, especially where new girls are concerned. It's just that we expect 'newies' to act like 'newies'; you know what I mean. For example, new girls normally creep into the classroom, looking helpless and slightly lost, then they wait to be told where to sit. That's where *we* come in, all helpful and friendly. I mean, people *need* friends when they are new to a place.

Not so with Amanda Pitkin-Smythe! Three days ago it was. In she marched, complete with leather briefcase and slimline skirt, *demanding* a seat near the window. By the end of that morning we all knew her life-history and her father's too. He is an ambassador somewhere or other . . . so she said.

She also told us that this was her tenth school. No wonder she was confident. New classrooms were just another footprint on the map to her.

As Jane whispered to me at the time, perhaps the other nine schools were glad to be rid of her.

Anyway, it did not take long for Amanda P-S to settle in; five minutes in fact. By the second day she was unbearable, really finding her feet, so to speak, and the rest of the class seemed to be quite taken in by her boasts. Several of the younger girls were following her around, hanging on her every word, even carrying books for her. And that was then the fan craze began.

Her father was travelling halfway round the world – can you blame him? – and he had sent her some real lace fans from Spain. She brought them to school and handed them out, keeping the biggest for herself. Hers was black and huge and handmade, and she really was in her element; waving it, wafting it, and doing that silent 'fan talk' which is just another way of Amanda-type showing off. It was a craze that really caught on. They were known as the Fan Gang.

But Jane agreed with me, that was the main thing. Amanda had to be put in her place and we were the ones to do it. And that was why I was spending my precious lunch break thinking murky thoughts. Murky, lurky thoughts about Amanda.

I lifted my head from the classroom window ledge and looked at Jane who, by now, was eating more crisps, bacon-flavoured this time. "Do you think we could get hold of a real fan?" I said, "only a bigger, better one than hers."

Jane nearly choked. "What, and show her that we really care? That would just be following the other poor sheep."

"Not really," I said. "If we could get hold of a better fan it would make hers look stupid by comparison."

Jane made another face, at me this time. "And where do we get a bigger, better fan? They don't come up with the daisies exactly."

"Well, what about the junk shops in town. They might have one tucked away," I said.

"Sure," nodded Jane. "Fans are selling like mad. There's a boom in the sale of fans this year, didn't you know?"

Sarcasm comes naturally to Jane and when she's in that sort of mood you can't win. So I gave the subject no more thought, well, hardly any thought, until home-time, when the flickering of twenty-odd fans goaded my mind to a new alertness.

"I've got it!" I shouted to Jane. "Your brother in the Navy."

"What about him?" she said, looking at me as if I had gone quite mad. "He's in the Far East right now."

"Exactly," I said, pulling aside to divulge my fan plan. She listened quietly and began to grin. "Good idea!" She thumped me on the back. "I'll write to him tonight and tell him to send two gigantic, gorgeous fans."

"And as quick as he can," I reminded her. "If he sends them by Air Mail we should get them within a week."

We managed to get through the next few days at school; the fan gang didn't annoy us quite so much with their oscillations now because we knew that our own fans would soon arrive.

We planned to make an entrance with them as soon as they came, and many a secret smile was shared as we imagined our plan in action. Not a word or a sign would we give the others until, hey presto, we would be flashing the biggest, gaudiest fans ever to leave the hot climes.

As it turned out the two fans arrived – wouldn't you know it – on a Saturday morning. It was awful having to wait through the whole of the weekend until we could really use them on the Monday morning.

Jane brought the box to my house and as we unpacked them from the tissue paper we both gasped in surprise.

Her brother had certainly 'shopped around'. They were big, much bigger than any of Amanda's crummy old fans. And they were made of silk brocade with fine bone handles. It is difficult to describe the colours, because the silk was shot through with a hundred other shades and hues, depending on which way it caught the light.

"Beautiful!" I sighed, as I picked one up and practised my eyelash-flutter, come-hither look over the top of it.

"Smashing!" said Jane, with complete lack of finesse. She fanned herself with a twisty wrist movement. "Just wait until Monday, the others won't believe their eyes!"

Well, as it happened, the others were not very interested on the Monday. As we arrived at the classroom door a new sound met our ears; not the usual flick-flutter sound, but a louder, harsher click-clack noise. Castanets!

Everyone, but everyone, was stomping round the room and making a heck of a din with painted castanets.

"Hello, you two," drawled Amanda Pitkin-Smythe. "Daddy sent me another parcel from Spain." She brandished a handful of castanet under our noses. A polished wood, magnificent castanet; kept the best for herself as usual! Her sickening voice went beefing on above the hub-hub, but we were hardly listening to her. We just stared, Jane and I. Stood and stared at all the girls as their faces showed distinct signs of castanet trance.

I was speechless.

And Jane? She took the box containing our precious fans and threw it to the floor. Then she danced on it, looking furious, almost dangerous! It was a strange, stamping dance full of hidden meaning. Something akin to a fantastic *fan*dango.

Put on your DANCING shoes

says Glynis Holland

So you want to be a ballet star? Well, it's one of the loveliest careers you could have.

And if you've really set your heart on ballet, if you know you have the talent to be successful and, very important, if you're prepared to work really hard — then the best possible way you could learn is to go to a ballet school.

We've found out about two of the best in Britain. . . .

BUSH DAVIES SCHOOLS

The famous Bush Davies School in Sussex has trained hundreds of talented dancers over the years, and students have gone on to leading ballet companies, film and television work, and commercial theatre.

The school is housed in the lovely old buildings of Charters Towers, set in twenty-two acres of the beautiful Sussex countryside. In the grounds, in contrast to the old buildings of the school, is the new and very modern Adeline Genée Theatre, which provides the perfect setting for the school's ballet productions.

Students at the school learn all about the ballet from highly qualified and experienced teachers, and the syllabus includes Character, Mime and Gesture, National Dance, Contemporary, Jazz, and Creative and Rhythm Tap.

There's a large music department too, as well as speech and drama

Early arrivals warming up in the Marjorie Davies Studio before theatre class

A scene from the ballet "The Emperor's New Clothes", performed at the Adeline Genée Theatre in 1971. The choreography was by the school's Principal, Miss Noreen Bush

Advanced Class practising in the Doreen Wells Studio

classes, and students are given every opportunity to develop these particular talents to the full.

Every aspect of stagecraft is taught, and there is plenty of practical work too, notably in the super productions staged in the Adeline Genée Theatre.

The students do all the work on these productions themselves, and you can see from our pictures just how good the results are.

But though the emphasis at the school is obviously on ballet and stage work, don't think that going to a ballet school lets you out of all your school work! There's an academic curriculum at the Bush Davies School too, and students aim for a minimum of five O-levels. This is very important of course, and those O-levels might well be invaluable later on, if you try for entrance to a college of further education.

Charters Towers have a day school too, in Romford, Essex, for those students who live within travelling distance.

If you'd like to find out more about the schools, you can write for prospectuses to: Bush Davies Schools, Charters Towers, East Grinstead, Sussex, and The Studio, 31 Eastern Road, Romford, Essex.

THE DANCE CENTRE

The London Dance Centre in Covent Garden is a quite remarkable kind of

A scene from Through the Cool and Out, *a modern work by Pat Whittock and performed at the Adeline Genée Theatre*

school.

It's an open school, which means that you can go in just for one or two hours a week, for an hour's lesson in the particular kind of dance you particularly enjoy. Each hour's lesson costs about 60 pence.

And there's an amazing choice of dance classes. Looking through the Dance Centre's timetable, there are classes in Classical Ballet, Tap, Jazz, Freestyle Modern, Yoga, Character, GoGo, Dance for Actors, Russian Ballet and Flamenco, to name but a few.

The classes are held in all grades too, from beginners to professional.

The Dance Centre's a wonderful place for young ballet enthusiasts. It's been brilliantly converted from a disused Covent Garden fruit warehouse, and it's now a bright, exciting place, where you can go to practise, buy books and costumes, have lunch or coffee, chat about ballet, and rub shoulders with dancers from leading companies, who often go there to rehearse. You might even be able to see a film being made — as there are facilities for filming too!

The teaching in the school is of the finest standard, and many of the teachers are known and respected all over the world.

If you'd like to find out more about this super school, write to: London Dance Centre, 12 Floral Street, London WC2E 9DH.

Practice at the barre for a class at the London Dance Centre, and some helpful advice for one of the girls from the class teacher

Poised perfection — a class at the Dance Centre practises this lovely position

Funny World!

The smallest independent country in the world is the Vatican City where the Pope lives as head of the Roman Catholic Church. The city receives money from Roman Catholics all over the world. As well as having its own telephone system and water supply, passports and stamps, the small state contains the largest Christian Church in the world. St Peter's was completed in 1612 and, with its gardens, covers most of the little country's area.

People used to think that the giraffe was a cross between a camel and a leopard and so they called it a Cameleopard.

The heaviest weight ever lifted by a man was by American Paul Anderson in 1957 when he lifted 2·8 tons, which is as much as a Rolls Royce complete with passengers!

'Sausage dog' is the nickname for the Dachshund, which has still kept the name the Germans gave to it, which means 'Badger hound'. But it is not a German dog, it was bred 4,000 years ago by the Ancient Egyptians.

Fine and Fancy

Remember the days when the shoe-shops were packed with pair after pair of the same old style, in a choice of basic black, or boring brown? And the time when tights were leg-coloured – and dull?

Well, it *was* like that once upon a time – but not any more! The shoeshop windows now are like exciting rainbows of super shades. And there are all those fabulous materials, too, from suedes and leathers, to wet look, canvas and even slinky velvets. There are wedge heels, chunky heels, peep toes, ankle straps, buckles and bows.

Here's a super line-up of fashion favour-ites in toning colours of suede. These three pairs of shoes are made by Saxone, Lilley and Skinner, and they would be an attractive and useful addition to any wardrobe.

How about this for trendy? This picture shows anyone who wasn't convinced, that tights just aren't dull any more! These side-patterned tights are by Wolsey, and the stripe effect has the added bonus of slimming down plump-ish legs.

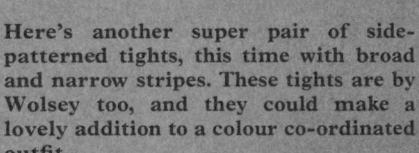

Here's another super pair of side-patterned tights, this time with broad and narrow stripes. These tights are by Wolsey too, and they could make a lovely addition to a colour co-ordinated outfit.

And as for tights. . . . Suddenly the shop counters are loaded with hundreds of different pairs, in so many pretty textures and tones. You can choose your tights to suit your clothes, and with clever use of accessories you can transform a plain dress into a stunning co-ordinated outfit.

And there's an added bonus these days, too. The manufacturers are constantly coming up with new hard-wearing yarns and weaves, and with care one pair of tights can last you for months.

Here's a super line-up of shoes, and some pretty textured tights. As you wander round your local shops you'll see that there are hundreds more to choose from. Buy carefully, with the rest of your wardrobe always in mind. But be a little adventurous with the new colours and styles. Try some fine and fancy fashions!

Are you SUPERSTITIOUS?

You may say you're not — but have you *never* crossed your fingers? Have you *never* carried a lucky charm? If not, then you are one of the few people in history who don't believe in the Lady Luck.

Fate, it would appear, cannot be changed, but your luck may be attracted by a word or a lucky mascot, and it can be turned against you by a careless action or the loss of the mascot. Often you may know that good or bad luck is coming your way because an omen lets you see the future. Many of the rulers of past days depended on omens and mysterious signs to tell them how to govern their countries.

The Romans, those mighty conquerors of the ancient world, employed unscrupulous fortune-tellers who claimed to see the future events by looking into the entrails of animals they killed for the purpose, and great decisions of state were made on the strength of what these butchers found. The Romans also believed that when they had a haircut a thunderstorm would rage in the sky that night!

The Kings and Queens of England have also been influenced by superstition. Queen Elizabeth I depended on a magician named John Dee whose magic stone was said to divine the future, and Henry VIII believed that he was trapped into falling in love with his second wife Anne Boleyn by witchcraft! Even the staid Queen Victoria once sent a tiny luck charm to a friend in the trust that it would protect him from 'all evil'.

Great businessmen, the people who would seem the most unlikely believers in superstition, are the most vulnerable nowadays. An American millionaire named Vanderbilt always slept with the legs of his bed standing in small bowls of salt to ward off the evil spirits, and J. D. Rockerfeller, the man who was said to be the richest in the world, set great store by an eagle stone, a small stone found in the nest of an eagle. Rockerfeller often presented people with a piece of the ribbon from which the stone was suspended, which as well as bringing luck to the recipient also saved the expense of buying a present!

The German dictator Adolf Hitler was guided in his tactics by astrologers and black magic, so perhaps we would have lost the Second World War had not our leader Winston Churchill stroked each passing black cat for good luck!

Perhaps the most amazing omen concerns the ill-fated Kennedy family of America. John F. Kennedy had been assassinated some years before, and

his younger brother, Robert Kennedy, and a Russian friend drank a toast that he might carry on the work of his brother. As is the custom in Russia, they threw down the glasses to smash them after the toast — and the frail glass refused to break. Some weeks later Robert too fell under the assassin's bullet.

Not only the rulers, but also the majority of their subjects are super-

stitious, although some of them are unwilling to admit it. The Maltese churches until only recently were built with two clock faces on their towers, one of which displayed the real time, and the other a different time to confuse the Devil who often lurked around on the Sabbath Day. In Iceland at one time a ghost who was troublesome could be tried before a court of law and ordered to keep the peace. In Japan an animal is an unwelcome visitor to a funeral. It is believed that the spirit of the person being buried will enter into the animal and it will become a vampire.

Perhaps the most superstitious country in the world today is Africa, where in some areas the witchdoctor is such a powerful figure that a general practitioner trained in the most modern methods of medicine cannot cure a man who has been told by the witchdoctor that he will die. The power of suggestion is so great that he usually *does* die — even though his illness was not serious. This tremendous power is also extended to Africans who come to study or work in Europe. Many have been known to pay large sums of money to the witchdoctors in the towns where they lived, as protection money to prevent the men of magic from casting evil spells upon them.

Of course, superstition is just nonsense. Or is it? Every race of the world has believed in witches, omens and lucky charms, and many still do. But if you are a sensible and modern thinking person you will reject these beliefs as foolishness.

But keep your lucky rabbit's foot, just in case!

Are you bewildered by the dazzling array of prettily-packed preparations on the beauty shop counters? And do you often find that the ones which promise the best results are just too expensive?

Well, don't despair. Here are some beauty products which you won't find on the make-up counters — but you might well find in the kitchen cupboard. . . .

Take the humble cucumber, for instance. When you've got five minutes to spare, cut some thin slices of cucumber — making sure that the particular cucumber you're cutting hadn't been especially bought for a salad at tea-time!

Lie down, and carefully put the thin slices all over your face. Peel them off after five minutes. The cool cucumber will have drawn all sorts of impurities from your skin, and will leave your face feeling clean and refreshed.

Fruit is also a valuable beauty aid, as well as being good to eat. If you have fair hair, try adding the juice of one lemon to your final rinsing water after you have shampooed your hair. It will bring out the highlights in your hair, and give it a super glossy sheen.

For darker hair, cold tea — yes, tea! — makes an excellent final rinse. But do remember to use tea bags — or carefully strain out all the leaves first!

Salt has numerous beauty uses, and here's an idea for one part of you which tends to be forgotten in the average beauty routine — your feet. If your feet are feeling tired after carrying you around all day, let them soak for a while in a bowl of warm water, to which you have added a handful of salt.

And try occasionally brushing your teeth with salt — it's not at all as bad as it sounds! Moisten your toothbrush, sprinkle on a little salt, and brush your teeth as usual.

To finish off with, here's one which you might not believe — but you'll have to try it to see if it works for you. It's yoghurt hair conditioner: not the fruit flavoured kind, just plain yoghurt. Use as a conditioner after shampooing, and rinse off with tepid water. Make sure that you rinse it *all* off! This is especially good for fine hair.

So next time you're at the beauty counters, pause before you buy that expensive preparation. You might just find that some of the best budget beauty products are in the kitchen cupboard!

BUDGET BEAUTY

THE YOUNG LOVERS

A Legend of Old China

In far-off days there lived in the Chinese province of Shuntang a rich and powerful mandarin. His house, set in gardens of great splendour, stood on a low hill overlooking the river Li and the fishing village which straggled along its banks.

The mandarin was a proud man. Every day he burned much incense and read many prayers to the spirits of his ancestors. But his greatest pride was his only child, a young girl whose beauty was already a legend in the valley of Shuntang. Her eyes were deep pools aglow with the light of a thousand stars; her hair was darker than night, while the fragrance of cherry blossom and the warm creaminess of tea-roses were mingled in her cheeks. She was lovelier than the dawn.

Her name was Lin-Si-Ling, which meant 'Tears of Moonlight' in the language of those days. Men came from all parts of the earth to pay homage to her beauty and to plead for her hand in marriage. The mandarin was well pleased by this, for he was ambitious and planned to unite his daughter with some old and powerful family.

But Lin-Si-Ling pleaded that she was yet too young for marriage, and begged that she might remain a little longer in the scented gardens of her father's house. And so it happened that she fell in love with Yen-Po-Weh, the fisherman. He was young, tawny-skinned, with eyes that glowed with tenderness and a smile like the glint of sunlight on a quiet pool.

He spent most of his time in the waters of the Li, for in the old-time speech the name Yen-Po-Weh meant 'Little Goldfish Without A Tail'. Often in the still afternoons he would stray beneath the high walls of the mandarin's gardens and sing of love to Lin-Si-Ling.

Sometimes he sang of life on the river: of enchanted gardens in the deep waters, where rainbow-coloured

by William Price

fish played hide-and-seek among strange flowers; of smooth wavelets that kissed the swimmer's face; of lizards asleep on the sun-baked mud-flats, and a choir of frogs who sang their croaking chorus to the stars.

The gentle Lin-Si-Ling was enthralled, and besieged by exciting emotions. With every visit of the young fisherman her love for him grew stronger and an urgent desire to share the freedom of his life burned within her heart.

One day the mandarin was called away to a remote part of the province and Lin-Si-Ling saw that her chance had come. She took off her robes of fine silk and donned the simple dress of a servant girl. When Yen-Po-Weh appeared, she scrambled over the high wall and slid, breathless but unhurt, into his waiting arms.

Hand in hand they raced down the hillside. The cherry blossom was in flower and the river Li lay asleep, like a golden dragon, in the valley of Shuntang.

Lin-Si-Ling found everything as the fisherman had said. They laughed and played together in the warm shallows, and dived again and again into cool, green caverns and deep mysterious pools.

Time went on, and the boy and the girl lay side by side in the soft river sand, talking and dreaming, until only thoughts passed between them

as the moon rose above the far mountains and twilight crept up from the sea.

As they lay silent in the blue and silver shadows, a great noise burst upon the night. Lin-Si-Ling sprang to her feet with a cry of alarm. Many lights flashed in the village and above the noise of hurrying feet and excited voices she heard her father's voice raised in anger and grief. Suddenly, she felt afraid.

But Yen-Po-Weh, the fisherman, stood as calm and cool as his silent-flowing river. Taking the trembling girl by the hand, he led her gently and without fear to the enraged and anxious mandarin.

Lin-Si-Ling was at once carried off to her father's house, crying of her love for the fearless fisherman and pleading that he might be treated with tenderness.

But the mandarin's pride was aroused and his anger knew no bounds. Yen-Po-Weh was severely beaten with bamboo staves and flung into his boat, which was then cast loose and left to drift down to the open sea.

For a short time the fisherfolk missed the merry laughter of Yen-Po-Weh, the 'Little Goldfish Without A Tail'; but the sun still gleamed on the river, there were fish to catch and children to feed, and so the

simple life of the village went on as before.

But in the gardens of the mandarin all was still. Lin-Si-Ling lay silent in the darkened house and the mandarin was sunk in despair. Not all his wealth and power could bring back the cherry blossom to those ice-pale cheeks, or put back the stars in those deep, sad eyes.

On the hillside the cherry trees were bare, the sunlight cold; no wind breathed across the mandarin's gardens and the white peacocks which once stalked so proudly about the smooth lawns, moved slowly and strangely as in a dream.

When she had recovered some of her former strength, Lin-Si-Ling walked again in her father's gardens. Her beauty was still great, but its warmth had fled. The drooping willows withered at her touch; she chilled the very flowers and at her approach even the friendly goldfish hid themselves in the warmest corner of their pond.

Long and earnestly Lin-Si-Ling kept her vigil on the high garden wall, and long and earnestly she prayed that her lover might come back.

One night of storm, when the moon rode high in the angry sky, a tremendous tide swept up the river from the distant sea. And the fisherfolk gazed in awe as the mandarin's daughter fled from her father's house and leapt across the foaming river, until she was caught up in its mighty torrent and carried out to sea.

For many years after this time, lovers who met by night on the banks of the Li told of a little goldfish without a tail, which played in the light of the moon, whose pale beams splashed on the water like falling tears. But those who looked without love in their hearts saw only a cold moon floating on the dark river.

All this was long ago. The gardens of the mandarin and the hill upon which they stood are long since dust, and even the province of Shuntang is no more remembered.

brighten up your bedroom

Flowers brighten up the dullest room, the only trouble is that they don't last very long, and who can remember to change the water? The answer to the problem could well be artificial flowers, but I don't mean the plastic daffodil variety, so you needn't groan and turn to the next page, not just yet anyway!

I'm sure you've all seen those pretty tissue creations in boutiques and craft shops, and then noticed the price and passed on by. You've probably even thought how easy they would be to make, if you knew just how. Well, I'm going to tell you.

This is all you'll need:

A pair of sharp pointed scissors.

Different colours of tissue paper *(you'll only need two sheets to make a big, big flower).*

Thick galvanised wire— *ironmongers sell this by the gauge, you'll need no. 12 or 14 for these flowers.*

Fine wire *— florists sell reel wire, or even fuse wire will do.*

Now cut your sheets of tissue paper into 10-inch squares and then put together ten or twelve squares, this is enough for one flower, and remember, you may use sheets of all the same colour or you may like to have a multi-coloured flower, in which case you may use sheets of toning colours—it's entirely up to you.

Fold the squares in half and then into quarters and finally fold over once more, so that you end up with a triangular shape. Now mark 4 inches up either side of your triangle and draw an arc in between, as shown in fig. 1, and then trim into shape.

When you spread this out you'll be able to see your flower taking shape already. Make two holes exactly in the centre, as shown in fig. 2, and then thread a length of fine wire through them, fig. 3.

By squeezing together at the base, you can make a funnel shape. Wrap the fine wire around this and include the stem of thick wire, as shown in fig. 4. You'll need some wire cutters to cut the wire to length—Dad will probably be able to help you there. You'll have to think carefully before you cut the wire—think about the height of your vase, this should be some guide to the length of the stems that you'll need—and remember, large flowers have large stems, they need them as we need our legs, to stop them from overbalancing, so do make them long enough or they'll just be top heavy and look silly into the bargain!

Once you have secured the flower head to its stem—and do make sure that it is quite secure—you don't want it to fall off the first time that someone touches it to admire it. You might like to wrap some green crepe paper around the wire and the stem so that it has a nice finish.

Now comes the difficult bit, you mustn't be heavy-handed if you're going to make a success of this. Pull down each layer and separate, carefully now, just one by one, as shown in fig. 5.

Finally, pull the centre petals back into a vertical position, separate and fluff them up a little, and this is what your flower should look like!

SO YOU WANT TO BE A NURSE?

There are some girls who know for certain the first day they play hospitals with their dolls that they want to be a nurse, but there are many others who feel that this satisfying and important career might be right for them if only they knew more about the qualities, qualifications and training which are needed to become a good nurse.

THE FIRST STEP

Any girl thinking of taking up nursing should ask herself, honestly, if she has a genuine liking for people, for all patients are people, and they look to a nurse for help and understanding during a period of illness and convalescence.

Good physical health is also essential to carry out the many duties on the wards, and a nurse must also be reliable, loyal, have a sense of humour and be able to obey the rules and accept the normal discipline of any smoothly running hospital.

The educational qualifications vary depending on the type of training you wish to take.

For those who prefer the practical side of nursing there is a two-year course which, when successfully completed, results in a person becoming a State Enrolled Nurse. For this a girl needs a good all-round education, although no special educational qualifications are required.

If, however, you choose to study to become a State Registered Nurse, which takes three years, you must have a minimum of three GCEs, one of which must be in English or History. In Wales, Welsh is substituted for English, and as requirements vary from hospital to hospital, it is best to write for specific requirements to the hospital of your choice.

CADETS, PUPILS AND STUDENTS

Training for both State Enrolled and State Registered Nurses begins at eighteen, but should you be eager to enter the world of nursing at an earlier age you may be lucky enough to gain entrance to a hospital which runs a Nursing Cadet Scheme.

Usually wearing some distinguishing clothing (two well-known hospitals call their cadets 'primroses' and 'pinkies' because of the colour of their dresses) the cadets do many useful jobs about the hospital. They may help out in the Physiotherapy Depart-

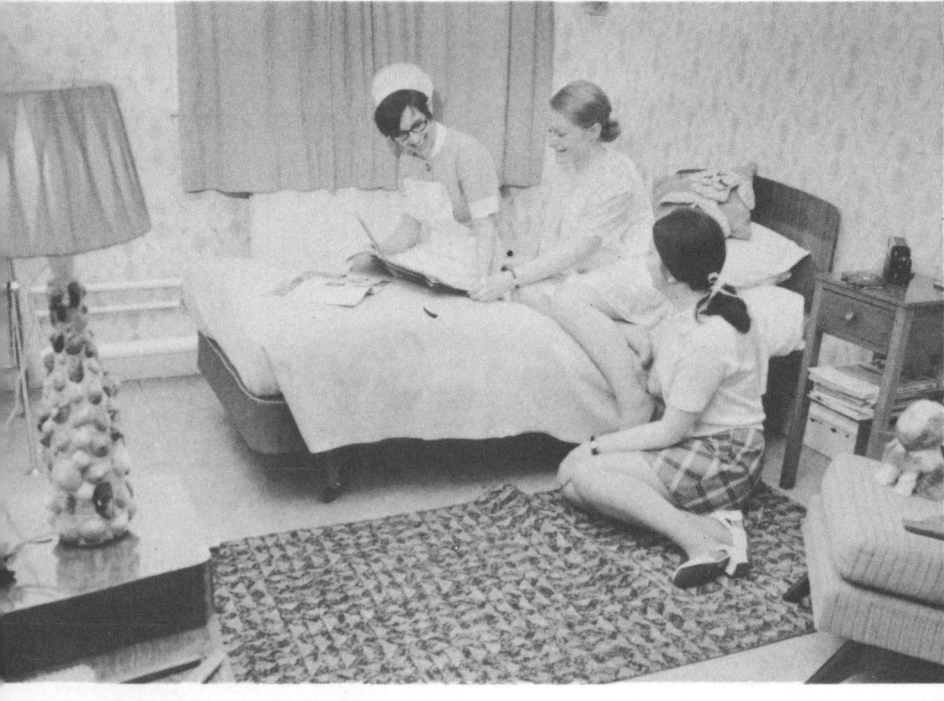

Friends can meet for a chat or to study in a comfortable study-bedroom.

Another helping hand with a jigsaw puzzle is always welcome.

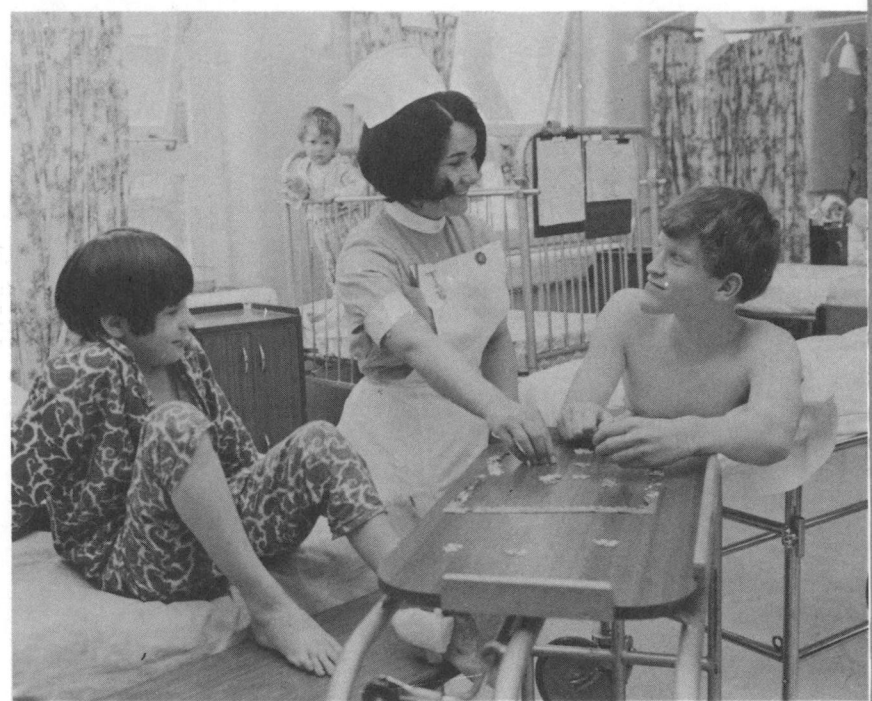

ment helping with patients' exercises; take telephone messages; prepare notes for clinics; help the pharmacy technicians to make up eyedrops and intravenous transfusion bottles; write letters for patients, and help to amuse the children of patients attending various clinics.

The Cadets are released from hospital duties for one or two days a week to attend a College of Further Education in order to study subjects which will help further their nursing career.

Some of these colleges themselves run pre-nursing courses, and should you be unable to enrol either at a hospital or a college, you can gain valuable nursing experience by joining the St. John Ambulance Brigade or the British Red Cross Society, as their courses cover a great deal of a nurse's first year.

As a Pupil Nurse, the future SEN practises on models during her first few weeks, and later training continues under qualified supervision so that there will always be someone there to help and advise about the correct procedure.

Skilled instruction is also given, both in the classroom and on the wards, by experts. During her second and final year the Pupil Nurse takes a practical test and, if successful, her name is entered on the Roll of Nurses and she is awarded her coveted SEN badge.

The training of an SRN Student Nurse covers both practical and theoretical nursing; the principles of medical and surgical treatment; the study of anatomy and physiology and the nature and causes of disease.

There is an eight-week introductory course during which the Student Nurse familiarises herself with the many different hospital departments, attends tutorials and makes visits to the wards.

Later she becomes a member of a Ward team, gaining practical experience under the expert guidance of her Ward Sister, while still attending tutorials for the theoretical side of nursing. There are also lectures by medical consultants, and sometimes the Student Nurse may be transferred to another hospital for a short time to gain experience in a speciality.

More responsibility is given to the final year Student Nurse, at the end of which the Hospital and State Final Examination leads to the State Registered Nurse qualification . . . the key to a varied and rewarding nursing career in hospital, abroad, or in industry.

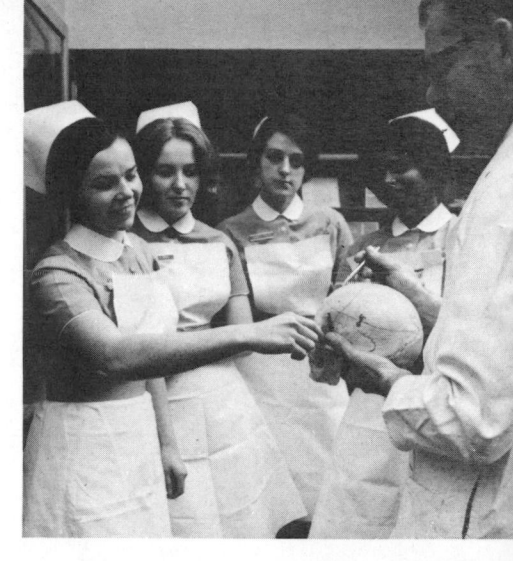

This skeleton head raises a smile, but he can be very instructive too.

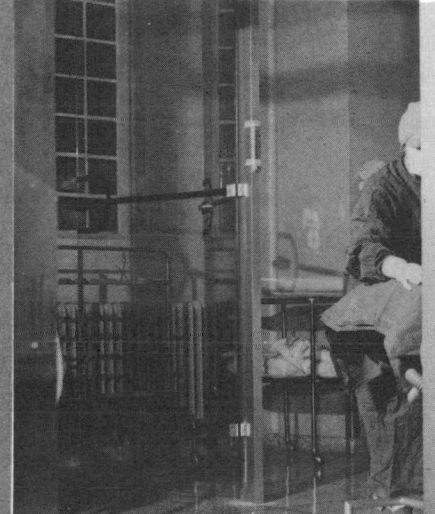

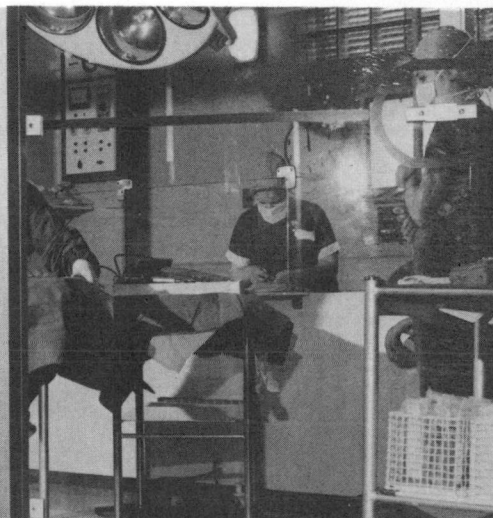

Getting the theatre ready for an operation requires skilled hands.

A happy moment for mother, baby and nurse in the maternity wing.

A nurse makes sure that an intravenous drip is working properly.

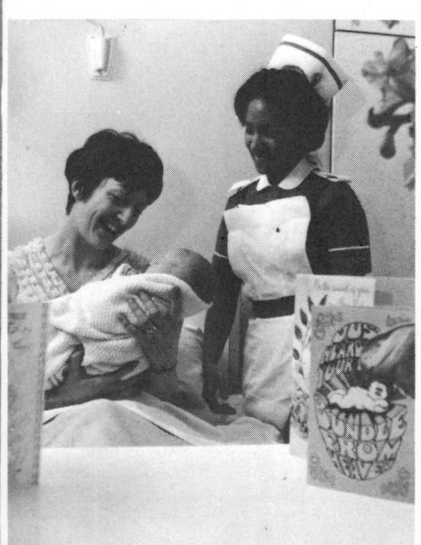

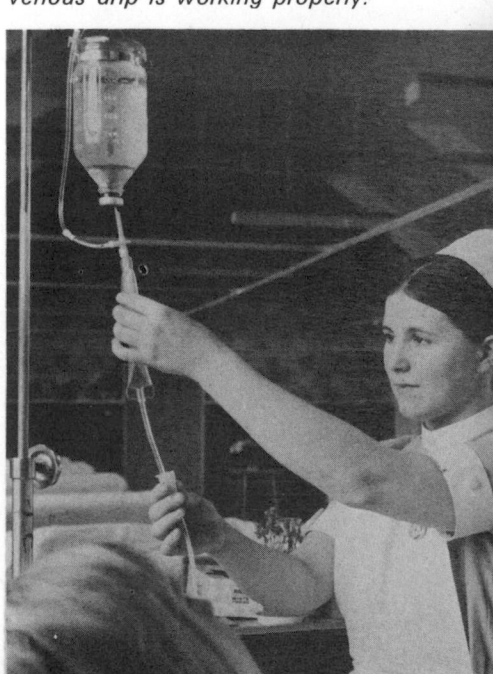

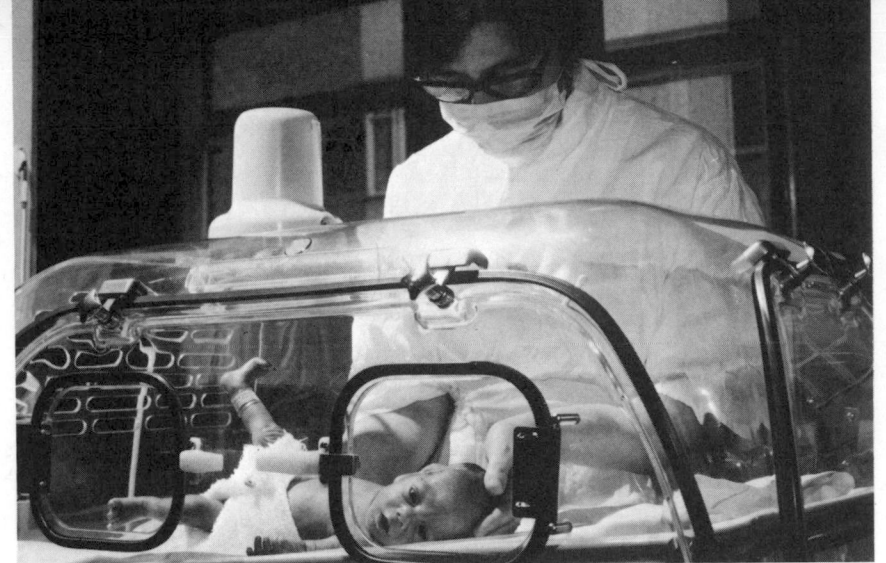

A tiny baby gets VIP treatment in an intensive care unit.

Medicine plays an important part in a patient's recovery, and all doses are carefully measured.

A smiling quartet of nurses agree that nursing is a satisfying, if demanding, career.

hospital for sick children two bright young student nurses were eager to speak of their work. They told of the enjoyment and satisfaction they got out of looking after the children in their care, bathing and feeding the babies, taking the children to and from the theatre and X-ray department and supervising meals.

A senior student nurse might be allowed to 'special' a patient, which meant that she was entrusted with looking after a child that needed special care and attention.

Students were also taken along on medical rounds to gain experience, and the whole hospital radiated with a warmth and friendliness which was apparent to every visitor.

A very experienced nursing sister there said that she had never seen a child really unhappy during its stay there throughout her time at the hospital.

But sometimes even the most skilled nursing is not enough, and a nurse must realise that nursing has its moments of sadness. A Nursing Tutor always tells prospective nurses that they must always ask themselves if they can face this fact without getting too emotionally upset. If they can, then nursing sick children is a very satisfying career.

ALL KINDS OF NURSING

But, of course, there are many other forms of nursing. You may like to train to become a Certified Midwife, or take a course in Opthalmic, Orthopaedic, or Thoracic Nursing.

Once qualified as an SRN you can become a District Nurse, School Nurse or train further to become a Health Visitor, as well as taking up interesting hospital posts such as Ward Sister, Staff Nurse or Nurse Tutor.

If travel appeals to you, you could join one of the armed forces, and see the world while looking after Servicemen and their families, or accept a short appointment overseas with the World Health Organisation or a similar international organisation.

Nursing can be a good life — and a very satisfying one!

SICK CHILDREN'S NURSING

One branch of nursing which may appeal to you provided you have patience, sympathy and a real love and understanding of children, is that of Sick Children's Nursing. At many hospitals girls can take an integrated four-year course in both sick children's nursing and general nursing, and so obtain a valuable qualification in two fields of nursing.

At one very well-known northern

If you want to know more about nursing and current conditions, rates of pay, holidays and so forth, write to the following addresses:
The Chief Nursing Officer,
Department of Health and Social Security,
Elephant and Castle,
London S.E.1.
The Nursing and Hospital Career Information Centre,
8, Leake Street,
London S.E.1.

ON A SPANISH HOLIDAY

by Catherine Morris
A friendship was formed, and a mystery was solved.

Once more my father consulted his road map.

"We must hit that town soon," he muttered, "and find a good hotel."

"Own up," said my mother. "We're lost. Your Spanish, like your other languages, is perfect – but your map reading is hopeless."

I felt it was all my fault, because it was my inability to speak Spanish fluently that had brought us to this isolated part of Northern Spain where few natives spoke English, and English tourists didn't come. So to survive I would be forced to practise my Spanish; only a teacher in Modern Languages like Dad could think up a thing like that.

"We turn here," proclaimed Dad. His turn led us into a narrow lane.

He braked violently because a foot away, astride his mule and flourishing his pitch-fork, was a Spanish peasant.

Apologising, my father asked the route to the town. Even I understood the old man's reply. There was no town. But there was a village, and we could stay at the *Alta Mira*.

"Well?" asked Dad.

"No choice," sighed Mum.

Dusk had fallen. The pine trees closed darkly around us. Suddenly we bumped along a cobbled street, and minutes later reached the village square. One side was gay with lights from small shops glowing with china, fans, embroidered cloths and mantillas in gold and silver thread. On the opposite side, in the shadows, stood tall grey mansions that had once housed nobility, as engraved coats-of-arms above the doorways proved.

It was like an opera scene. Next the chorus would dance in. But instead a peasant drove his cows across to a dark side street.

"Not even an inn," said Mum crossly. "Wake up, Sally."

Then I saw the solitary light in the shadows ahead of us, and the faint words – *Alta Mira*.

"Over there," I cried, pointing. "There's *Alta Mira*."

"Good!" exclaimed Dad. "At least the place exists."

We parked, and then went through the crooked gate. Ahead lay a tangled garden. Large lily-shaped flowers gleamed ghost-like on clumps of trees. Mum stopped to smell one.

"Come on," said Dad impatiently. "Forget the Botany."

A rough stone path led to a court-yard, and there on three sides stretched *Alta Mira*.

A bright light above an ancient, heavy half-open door showed the heraldic arms of some mediaeval Spanish nobleman.

Silently we entered a long room floored in marble, with a reception desk and a bar at one end. On the other under a Moorish arch were small cafe tables, and between soared a marble staircase which disappeared into oak panelling.

"Do we ring?" Mother sounded over-awed.

Staring up at the panelling I saw

a square move. Then an eye peered down at us from the panelling. A second later a smiling Spaniard ran down the stairs to welcome us, and a small peasant boy was called to guide us to our rooms.

Though the grounds of this palace converted to a hotel were neglected, the interior had a well-kept, mysterious dignity. All the floors were of marble. There seemed to be miles of dark-panelled corridors, and where oak yielded to stone, old tapestries hung. Swords and ancient fire arms decorated corners, and real suits-of-armour stood in the most unexpected places. Grilles of fine iron-work let in light in some passages, providing views of the floors below. The more I saw the more excited I became.

After countless twists and turns my small guide produced a huge key, and opening a creaking door ushered me into an ante-chamber furnished with dark, carved cupboards. A grille overlooked the staircase. Then, producing another large key, he showed me into my bedroom, and left me.

The big bed and the massive furniture were very old. The only modern touch was my bathroom, complete with bath and shower.

Later we dined in what must have been a ballroom in a past age.

The head waiter, armed with a menu and a wine list, brought with him a well-groomed boy. Bowing he said, "Welcome, Senor Wyatt, Senora and Senorita. Because you are English I give you my English student as waiter."

I nearly laughed out loud. My father's idea was that I should order all the meals in Spanish to practise the language. I expected him to explode.

Instead he replied in his perfect Spanish, "Thank you, Senor. But to become fluent in Spanish my daughter must speak your language at table."

"Or starve!" I murmured under my breath.

The English student gave me a sympathetic look, and I thought that he didn't look English. With black hair and olive skin he looked Spanish.

Spaniards are always gay in the

late evening, and after dinner the *Alta Mira* bar and café were very busy. Out in the square music blared and villagers were dancing.

"Let's go shopping," said Mother. "I'd like hand embroidered cloths and a mantilla."

The tablecloths were fabulous and the mantillas dreamy, but as we crossed the square I'd spied a junk shop lurking in the shadows near the old mansions. Such shops fascinate me, especially if like this one they display old swords in the window. So while Mum and Dad were engrossed with refined embroidery I worked my way quietly to the door. Once outside I dodged the dancers and entered the junk shop.

Inside there was a smell of old leather. Nothing was arranged. Old agricultural equipment was dumped here, and domestic utensils there. I made for a tangle of old swords and daggers. This purchase would have to be kept secret so I chose an old dagger – really old, not imitation – that would fit into my shoulder-bag.

The owner of the shop was gossiping when I asked him the price in Spanish. Then I haggled over the price because I knew that I was expected to bargain.

The man's companion laughed, and said in English, "If that is not fluent Spanish what does your Father call fluent?"

And there, grinning, stood our English student waiter. He spoke rapid Spanish to the storekeeper who laughed and said, "Senorita, for a friend of the Senor's I sell to you at half-price."

Having paid, I waited while the dagger was ceremoniously wrapped.

The student said, "I'm John. I know you're Sally, and that your Spanish is very good."

I smiled replying, "Only when I'm not conscious of being criticised. Please don't say you saw me here or mention the dagger." Then I asked, "Are you really English? You look so Spanish."

John looked at me intently. Then he said, "I'll swop my secret for yours. I won't tell you bought a dagger in a junk shop, and you won't tell anybody that my mother's Spanish. Her father left this village in a

hurry a long time ago. Nobody here knows that I'm his gradson. Nobody must know."

"Why tell me?" I asked quietly.

"Because I like you, and because somehow I feel you can help me. Get back now to wherever you're supposed to be. We'll talk again."

I nodded, and thanked the junkman. Then, with my dagger snug in my shoulder-bag, I slipped across the square, and was in the embroidery shop doorway as my parents were coming out.

In bed that night I went over

John's strange remarks. Why had his grandfather left this village in a hurry? Was he a criminal? What was John up to that had to be kept secret, and how could I help? And how and where could I meet John to get answers to these puzzling questions?

I felt a little scared, but strangely excited. I'd read somewhere once that some places are made for mysteries. *Alta Mira* seemed to me to be such a place, and now I was to be part of it.

Next morning Mum, Dad and I

explored the foothills of the Pyrenees in the cool of the day.

Free of *Alta Mira* I wondered if I'd dreamt the visit to the junk shop and that talk with John. But the weight of the dagger in my shoulder-bag was real enough.

We returned for lunch, and then when it became hotter, my father read under the lily-trees, and Mum went to bed.

Now I was able to explore the old palace, and to check if there were any more peepholes. I tested all the panelling I could politely search, and so it was that I found a spy-hole that overlooked the library.

Below me an old writing-table set with writing materials gleamed with the polish of centuries. The library walls were lined with richly bound leather books, and there was John taking down book after book – not reading but peering into the emptiness the book had filled. Silently I

slid back the panel. I decided that this was the time and place to have my talk with John.

He was so intent on his search that he didn't hear me enter. I touched him on the shoulder. He spun round.

"You!" he exclaimed thankfully.

"Did you know there's a spy-hole above?" I asked. "That's how I found you."

John stared. "Let's sit down," he said.

I glanced round. "In that corner," I pointed. "That's not in the spying focus." We sat, and I waited.

"Last night," said John, "after you'd gone I thought I'd been wrong asking you to help me. Now you've proved me right. I never thought of checking up on peepholes. I need you, Sally."

Now he waited.

"Tell me the whole story," I suggested. "Why your grandfather left; why your relationship must be a secret, and what you're trying to find? It's obvious that you're searching for something."

"You've heard of the Spanish Civil War," said John. "My grandfather was the son of this house. He fought on the losing side. He wasn't a Communist, but he believed that this province should rule itself."

"I'm with you so far," I said.

"My grandmother and my mother – a baby – had already left. They were smuggled over the Pyrenees, and I presume my grandfather in his turn used the same route. When my mother was four years old grandmother died and grandfather, now alone, sent my mother to stay at the Convent of the Holy Virgin. A year later he died, and the nuns cared for Mother till she was sixteen. Then she left for a job. When she left the nuns gave her a letter Grandfather had written eleven years before – It's the conclusion of the letter that's important to me. It said that in *Alta Mira* was hidden a family heirloom – an emerald cross given to an ancestor by Philip II of Spain. It was now Mother's. Then he wrote, 'Let the Holy Virgin guide you always.' Mother's home had been the Convent of the Holy Virgin. I suppose he wanted her to remember the teachings of the nuns. And that's the end."

"Wasn't there any clue where the cross was hidden? In the beginning of the letter perhaps?" I asked.

"Nothing." John shrugged hopelessly.

"Somebody could have found the cross and said nothing." I suggested. "Emeralds are worth a fortune."

"I've thought of that," replied John miserably. "But I've got to try. I can't ask the old villagers how he left. They'd guess I was connected, and politically the family are suspicious characters."

I sat thinking. John watched me.

"There were alterations when this palace was converted into a hotel," I said slowly. "Like my bathroom. So the cross if it's here, would be in the untouched parts."

"Right," agreed John.

"If I were leaving for good I'd have that heirloom on me," I argued.

"But suppose at the last minute I realised that an enemy was lying in wait and that I might be caught and searched, I'd hide it as I was leaving."

"That makes sense," said John. "But it's all supposition."

Ignoring John I continued, "Which is the least exposed way out? Not the entrance hall."

"The side door from the interior cobbled patio," replied John promptly. "It's the servants' entrance. Dark with old cupboards. Thanks, Sally, I'll try there now."

"Don't forget the tops of the cupboards," I cautioned. "That's where people hide things."

By now I was as keen as John was on finding that emerald cross. I even

furtively searched a couple of suits-of-armour, peering down inside with a torch. I thought of secret hide-aways in the old panelling which lined corridors and rooms. But the more I puzzled, the more hopeless John's quest seemed.

At dinner that evening I caught John's eye, and raised my eyebrows. He shook his head slightly. So he'd had no luck in the cobbled patio.

Later during the meal the wine waiter ordered John to get my father a bottle of vintage wine from the old cellar. I pricked up my ears. Of course the old cellar. I could hardly wait to pass this idea to John. And while my parents were having coffee upstairs I excused myself, and caught

John clearing away the dinner things.

"Try the old cellar," I whispered, and fled as the head waiter approached.

John never served breakfast, so next morning thinking the servants' patio would be by the kitchens I went there, hoping John would see me. But the kitchens were the other side.

Near the patio was a sunken garden. I wandered in. It was an eerie place. The blank walls of the old palace rose above it. I felt a prickle of excitement. Here a hunted man could feel alone and unobserved. I waded through the tall grasses. Suddenly I stumbled against a curb. I held my breath because there hidden amidst the weeds stood a little Madonna with the Holy Child in her arms and a lamb at her feet.

John's grandfather had written, "Let the Holy Virgin guide you always."

This Holy Virgin, not the Convent of the Holy Virgin.

Desperately I pushed my fingers into the gap between the lamb's nose and the Virgin's skirts. I dug out dirt and dead leaves, and then a stained, softly-padded leather case.

I reached the privacy of my room safely and, locking the door, opened the case. There it lay, a cross of green fire set in gold, fashioned by some forgotten Spanish craftsman four hundred years ago.

A knock at the door startled me. There stood John.

"Your parents are having coffee"

he began.

"Oh John!" I cried. "I've found it." And I thrust the package into his hands.

"How? Where?" he stammered.

"It was easy," I said laughing. "I did what your Grandfather said: let the Holy Virgin guide me."

Then I told John of the lonely sunken garden, and the tiny shrine to the Holy Virgin.

"And Mother and I thought Grandfather meant that she must always follow the teaching of the Convent of the Holy Virgin," marvelled John.

"So did I," I said. "We all underestimated your Grandfather. His letter held the clue after all."

THE SECOND GENERATION

One of the zingiest, most talented groups in show business today is Dougie Squires' Second Generation, known more familiarly to their fans these days as the "2Gs". Not only are they a familiar name in British television, but they have also appeared in Germany, had their own charity cabaret spot and appeared in a Royal Gala Performance before H.M. The Queen and Prince Philip.

MEET THE GANG

As a group the 2Gs are simply terrific, as their fan mail shows, but since many of you are fans of a particular member of the gang, here's a chance to get to know them better.

Several members of the 2Gs were originally with the Young Generation before they joined Dougie Squires' scintillating Second Generation.

Heart-throb Bobby Bannerman started his acting career as naughty William in the BBC's *Just William* series and he was only twelve when he appeared with Claire Bloom in *Anna Karenina*. Since then he has made more than three hundred TV appearances, and Bobby is now a member of the 2Gs' 'Splinter', a small vocal group used on special occasions which features Bobby, Jeremy, Sandy and the two Lindas.

But all work and no play is not much fun, so Bobby recently flew to Corfu for a holiday with the two Rogers and

Rhys Nelson.

Roger Howlett, who has appeared in many TV shows, has a recording contract with Phillips. One of his popular releases is *One Love*, and Roger has also toured with shows like *My Fair Lady* and *Camelot*.

Roger Hannah, a few years younger than his namesake, has also had a taste of show business before joining the Young Generation. He has appeared in pantomime and has completed a summer season at Southend with the Dallas Boys.

A founder member of the Young Generation, Rhys left for a time to appear in two West End shows, but returned later and joined the Second Generation.

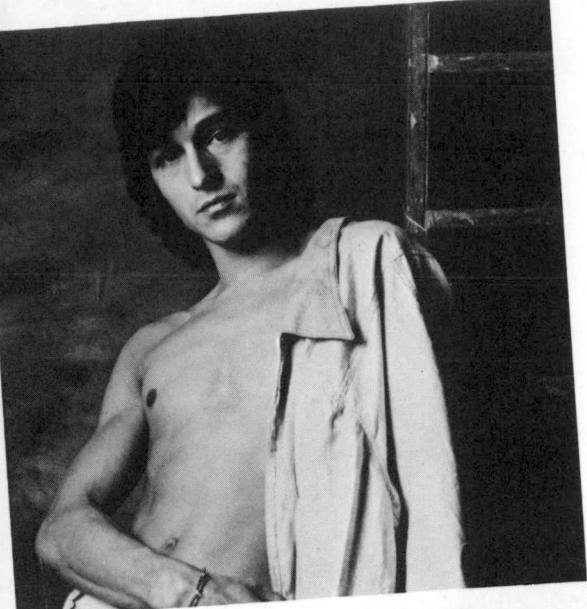

2.

ROMANTIC TWOSOMES

Two couples have found romance among the music. Sandy Penson and Brian Rogers now share a real-life partnership as well as a workaday one.

As well as working with the group, Brian has appeared with such show-biz personalities as Sandie Shaw, Lulu and Ken Dodd.

He loves sport of any kind, particularly football, and he is absolutely crazy about cars . . . but he hates dirty ones!

Sandy, his wife, loves archaeology and crocheting, and she absolutely adores old musical films starring folk like Gene Kelly and Fred Astaire. And, now that she has conquered the habit herself, Sandy hates seeing badly bitten nails!

Before auditioning for the Young

2. Handsome Bobby Bannerman in a thoughtful mood.

3. Roger Howlett has a recording contract with Phillips, so look out for his latest release.

4. A founder member of the YGs, Rhys Nelson has appeared in *Sweet Charity* at the Prince of Wales theatre.

5. Roger Hannah found that he enjoyed his spell in pantomime with Ted Rogers.

3.

5.

4.

Generation, green-eyed Sandy worked in Scottish TV and also abroad. It was Brian who suggested the audition and Sandy realised just how lucky she was to be accepted when she saw the other fifty people who were waiting!

Another member of the family is Bindi, a beautiful little Yorkshire terrier . . . it must have been a case of love me, love my dog, I suppose!

Another married twosome are Jeremy Robinson and Linda Jolliff.

Jeremy had a lucky break when Spike Milligan asked him to appear on his radio show . . . Spike even wrote two songs specially for Jeremy to sing. Look out for Linda as a member of the 2Gs' Splinter singing group. It promises to be something rather special. Perhaps you also saw Linda in ITV's *Please Sir* comedy series, or saw her in the touring version of *Hello, Dolly!*

9.

6 and 7. Despite their busy life in the Second Generation, Jeremy Robinson and Linda Jolliff found time to marry, and they enjoy their leisure hours together.

8. Pretty Ann Chapman was in a Gene Kelly movie and probably picked up a few tips from the dancing master.

9. Sandy Penson met Brian Rogers in Scotland and he persuaded her to audition for the Young Generation. Later, these two Second Generation dancers married last year.

8.

6.

7.

10.

11.

13.

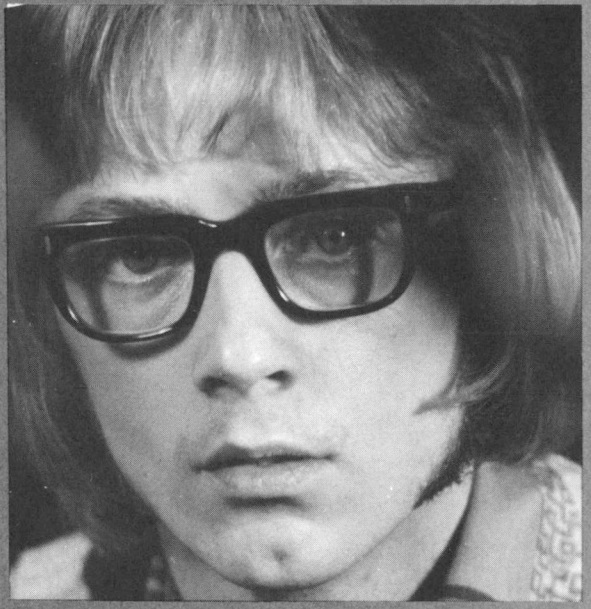

12.

10. Brian is the Captain of the 2Gs' football team, and supports the two teams in his home town of Sheffield.

11. Richard Gough, a talented member of the 2Gs, spent some time in his varied career touring Europe and the Middle East with a modern dance company.

12. In his spare time groovy Danny Grover likes "messing about in boats" on the River Thames.

13. Cheryl St. Clair spent her holiday on a cruise to Athens, and came back looking even prettier than usual.

PERSONALITY PARADE

You may have seen several of the 2Gs among the cast of many well-known musical shows. After playing Dickie Henderson's son on TV over eight years ago, young Danny Grover has appeared in *Fiddler on the Roof* at Her Majesty's theatre, and in *Poor Horace* at the Lyric theatre.

Chris Hennen has worked with those two very funny comedians, Morecambe and Wise. He has ap-

15.

14.

16.

14. A member of the group who believes that practise makes perfect is Peter Newton—he spent his holiday taking dancing lessons!

15. When he is not rehearsing these days, you'll find Chris Hennen at the piano . . . songwriting.

16. Linda Laurence is a member of the 'Splinter' vocal group, the group within the group.

17. As well as being a talented member of the 2Gs, Carolyn Heywood is also a prolific songwriter and keen guitar player.

peared in pantomime with Jimmy Tarbuck and you might have seen him in the popular TV series *Dr. Finlay's Casebook*.

It may seem a far cry from teaching dance movement at the Bristol Old Vic to appearing at fashion shows, but these are only two phases of Richard Gough's varied activities, which also include a period at the London Palladium . . . and even a spell at Harrods. Obviously, variety is the spice of life for talented Richard!

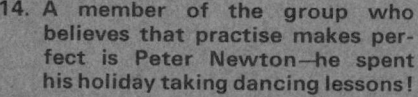

17.

18. Wei Wei Wong is one of the most popular members of the 2Gs and has very many fans who follow her career with interest.

19. A happy, gay routine for the 2Gs, but one which still needs plenty of practise.

20. Sometimes the 2Gs use an outdoor location for one of their dance routines.

A BEVY OF BEAUTY

But the story of the 2Gs would not be complete without a mention of some of the very talented girls

These include guitar-playing Carolyn Heywood who has worked with Lionel Blair and appeared in *Desert Song*; Radio One Girl Linda Lawrence, who loves dancing but hates knitting; pretty Cheryl St. Clair, and Ann Chapman who appeared in the Gene Kelly movie *Les Demoiselles de Rochefort*.

One of the 2G girls with a great fan following is Wei Wei Wong. Her record *Sing Song Boat* is sure to please you all!

If you would like to join the 2Gs' fan club, and get all the latest information and pictures about your favourite group, plus advance information about new record releases, plus special preference for tickets for their shows, write to:

**FAN CLUB SECRETARY,
C/O TRENDS MANAGEMENT,
59, GEORGE STREET,
LONDON W1.**

18.

19.

20.

Girls who go places

'Welcome to Spitalgate'. New WRAF recruits on arrival at the basic training camp

Are you looking for a career which will be a whole new way of life, where the emphasis is on team work, where there are good opportunities for promotion, and where there is the possibility of travel overseas?

If you've answered 'yes' to all those questions, the Women's Royal Air Force may well be the career for you.

In the WRAF you'd be working alongside men of the RAF. And for every RAF man flying, it has been calculated that 30 or 40 men and women are needed on the ground to do all the various jobs which are so vital to the smooth running of the Service. So you can see there's plenty to do.

If you're accepted for training as an airwoman in the WRAF you'll go first to RAF Spitalgate in Lincolnshire, on an initial six weeks' recruit training. Here you'll begin to learn something of the traditions and history of the Service you've joined, and something of the new life you are going to lead.

You'll meet some of the girls you'll be working with, and the training officers at Spitalgate will tell you all about your new career and will be glad to answer all the questions you may have. But remember. RAF Spitalgate is a training camp and you will be expected to work jolly hard.

After this six weeks' course, you'll be posted to a station where you'll begin your trade training. But in between the time you leave Spitalgate and the time you start your trade training you are given a week's leave, so you can visit home and tell your parents and your friends how you're getting on. Once you start trade training your new career will really be beginning.

AT THE STATION

Royal Air Force stations are bright, lively places, attractively furnished, centrally heated and with many recreational facilities.

Your quarters, by the way, will be smart and comfortable. You will share a room to begin with, but later you

A discussion group at an Officer Cadet Training Unit

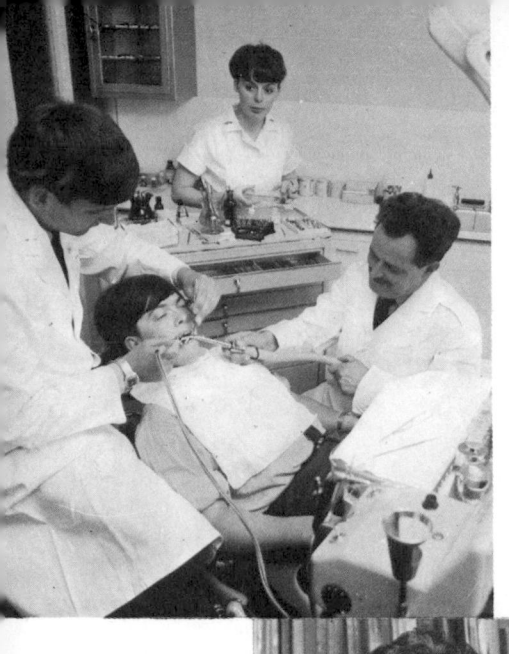

Dental assistant helping in the surgery

A WRAF officer of the Education Branch helping in the station library

may have one to yourself. Either way you can be sure it will be warm and well furnished, with attractive and practical furniture. And you can add your own personal touches with lampshades, bright cushions, pictures, etc. Or if you live near an RAF station operating the local service scheme you can work on the station each day and still live at home.

But if you choose to live on the station, and many girls do, you will be encouraged to take part in the many activities and clubs that exist. At the same time you are free to go into town to a dance or a show.

Women's Royal Air Force girls wear attractive uniforms, as you can see in the pictures, but uniform is only compulsory for working hours, the rest of the time you can follow all the latest fashion fads that you fancy.

BECOMING AN OFFICER

If your aim from the start is to become an officer in the WRAF you can apply for a commission from the ranks, or if you're eighteen you can apply for a commission straight from civilian life. You will need at least five GCE 'O' levels, including English, and either mathematics or a science subject. Those are the academic qualifications – but you will also require a good deal of self-reliance, initiative and readiness to accept responsibility. If you've got these qualities already, you're well on the way.

THERE'S WORK TO BE DONE

But what exactly will your work be in the WRAF? Well, there's an amazing variety of branches you can choose from, all of them vital parts of the RAF organisation as a whole. Here, briefly, are some of the jobs to be done.

Men and women in the Telecommunications branch work with messages which come by radio, teleprinter and telephone, signals from other bases in Britain, or from wherever the RAF serves overseas.

Maybe you're interested in catering? Well, every day there are thousands of hungry men and women to be fed with appetising, nourishing meals, in the pleasant surroundings of the mess dining hall. You could help with this big job.

An off-duty scene at a station's discotheque

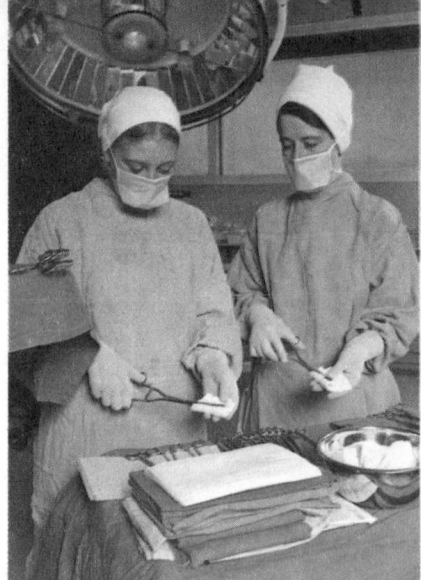

Nurses at PMRAFNS Hospital, Wroughton, prepare for an operation

Different again is the exciting and rewarding job of Air Traffic Control — working in the control tower providing invaluable in-flight information to aircrew. But don't worry — no one's going to expect you to do this job till you've learnt all there is to know about it.

Then there are the branches of General Service, Safety and Surface — which includes maintenance of vital equipment like parachutes and flying clothes — Engineering Trade Groups, Accounting and Secretarial, and Supply.

If you join the Mechanical Transport branch you will have the chance to drive almost every type of mechanical vehicle in RAF service.

In the Air Defence Operating branch you'll be observing aircraft using the most sophisticated and up-to-date radar equipment in the world.

There are opportunities too in the medical and dental branches of the service, working as receptionists, assistants, technicians or on clerical duties.

Something you may not have thought of is combining the two careers of nursing and the Royal Air Force, and you can do this in the Princess Mary's Royal Air Force Nursing Service.

And if your real ambition is to fly in jet aircraft of the Royal Air Force then there are opportunities for you to qualify as an Air Load Master, where you would be directly responsible for the supervision of aircraft loading and the safety of passengers and cargo.

So you can see that the variety of jobs in the WRAF is really tremendous. If any of these jobs appeals to you, go along to your local RAF careers information office and find out more. There are branches in most large towns, and they'll give you information leaflets which you can study at your leisure at home.

If there isn't an information office within easy reach of your home, write to the Inspectorate of Recruiting, Government Buildings, London Road, Stanmore, Middlesex, HA7 4PZ.

If the WRAF's the career for you, you might soon be off to a fine start.

Air Traffic Controllers lead an 'all action life'

"Would you care to order, sir?" A WRAF stewardess at an Officers' Mess

The Attestation ceremony — now you are part of the RAF organisation

ALICE IN WONDERLAND

Dormice in teapots, white roses painted red, playing cards that talk, and White Rabbits with pocket watches — where else could you be but in Wonderland?

A Wonderland created in the nineteenth century by a mathematician called Charles Lutwidge Dodgson, better known as Lewis Carroll. He first told the story of the adventures of Alice in Wonderland to the three young daughters of the Dean of Christ Church, Oxford, one of whom was called Alice. And it was six-year-old Alice Liddell who persuaded her favourite storyteller to write the tales down for her. It was an original Christmas gift, which the author had illustrated himself, and also it turned out to be a lucrative one — for this manuscript was sold for £15,000 seventy years later.

That 'memory of a summer's day', as Lewis Carroll called it, has lingered on and on and, as with most popular books, it finally became a film, well several films in actual fact, including a cartoon version from Walt Disney. But that's another story. . . .

The latest screen version, with its star-studded cast, is the one we're going to feature here, and it's certainly one of the most authentic film versions of the well-loved book.

INTO WONDERLAND

It all begins on one of those summer days, when it seems that the whole world has been lulled into a half-sleep by the warm sun, and nobody wants to move too much because it's such an effort. Mr Dodgson, alias Lewis Carroll played by Michael Jayston in

Alice — in Wonderland — where else . . . ?

Of course, it's all his fault; if Alice had never seen the White Rabbit she'd never have ended up in Wonderland. But then there wouldn't have been a story, would there?

Sir Ralph Richardson as the Caterpillar. In the film he has to sit on a ten-foot high toadstool smoking a pipe. But there was some consolation — he had it filled with his favourite tobacco!

Two guesses whose tea party this is. . . .

"Will you walk a little faster?" said a whiting to a snail.
"There's a porpoise close behind us, and he's treading on my tail.
See how eagerly the lobsters and the turtles all advance!
They are waiting on the shingle — will you come and join the dance?"

Alice meets the Mock Turtle and the Gryphon, and does, indeed, join the dance.

the film, is just beginning one of his tales of Alice for Alice Liddell and her sisters. Slowly Alice's eyelids begin to droop and slowly, slowly she drifts off until. . . . !

There's a roaring rush and there goes the White Rabbit, looking anxiously at his pocket watch as he scurries off. Of course, white rabbits aren't such a common occurrence — but white rabbits with pocket watches — well, that's a different matter altogether, I think you'll agree. So naturally, Alice follows, and it's no easy task following a scurrying white rabbit, especially *the* White Rabbit. And, it's even more difficult when you fall down a well in the process. But if that's the only entrance to Wonderland, then down you must go. . .

When Alice finally lands, however, the White Rabbit has completely disappeared from sight, leaving her quite alone in a beautiful hall with lots and lots of doors, and on the only table a solitary gold key: a key which will open only one door, a tiny one behind a curtain which leads into a beautiful garden, the most beautiful garden that Alice has ever seen. Trouble is, Alice is much too big to get through the door, and when she drinks a delicious mixture from a bottle labelled DRINK ME, she's too small to reach back onto the table for the key to unlock the door.

And so it goes on, and at one stage she's so tiny that she almost drowns in the tears that she wept when she grew to be nine feet tall. And that's where she meets the dormouse, who's swimming for his life . . . complicated, isn't it? Well, perhaps you'd better

Who stole the tarts? Well, whoever it was, the Queen's solution is to chop off his head!

read the book, or see the film, or better still, do both!

Otherwise how will you ever meet the Gryphon and the Mock Turtle, and the Mad Hatter, and the King and Queen of Hearts, and the Cheshire Cat, and the Duchess and the Caterpillar, and the March Hare . . . and how

will you ever find out how it all ended?

Among the people who did find out were the people who stepped into the roles of the magical characters of Lewis Carroll's imagination. People like Fiona Fullerton, who was chosen by Will Sterling, the Director, from over two hundred girls to play the role

Alice in that beautiful garden that she first saw through a tiny door.

Tweedledum and Tweedledee resolved to have a battle — you probably know the rest!

of Alice. She's a pupil at the Elmhurst Ballet School, Camberley, where Hayley Mills was once a star pupil, and Fiona made her first film debut in 1968. If you've seen *Nicholas and Alexandra* then you may remember her as Anastasia, the Tsar's youngest daughter.

A good many of the stars in *Alice in Wonderland* are completely unrecognisable, thanks to the success of their costumes and makeup. Michael Crawford, who plays the White Rabbit, spent two hours every day being transformed for his part, and throughout the film he is covered from head to toe in a white fur suit, complete with long floppy ears and a rubber face mask. You'd just never guess who the actor was under all that lot, if you hadn't been let in on the secret. . . .

And who would have guessed that the Cheshire Cat's head which grins from ear to ear is actually Roy Kinnear — and he's an electronic cat into the bargain! For in the story of *Alice in Wonderland* the Cheshire Cat has to wave its tail about whenever it's mad — and it's that waving tail that's electronically controlled. All Roy Kinnear had to do was to press a button and his tail would move gently in any direction required!

Imagine all that, together with a cast that includes Spike Milligan, Dudley Moore, Dennis Price, Sir Ralph Richardson, Michael Hordern, Hywel Bennett, Robert Helpmann, Davy Kaye, Dame Flora Robson, Peter Sellers, Rodney Bewes and, of course, all the others who've been mentioned, and you'll have some idea of that topsy-turvy Wonderland which Alice visits.

Why not try a visit yourself; read the book and see the film. There's no telling what you might discover. . . .

A Joseph Shaftel Production

Alice; always too big or too small, until she meets the Caterpillar. . . .

Looking at History

A report, by Gudrun Heatley, on the creation of historical costumes

It's quite difficult to understand the popularity of all the historical dramas on television, especially when you think that most people claim that they hated history at school . . . and when you look at some history text books it's easy to understand why. Perhaps, this is where the secret of television serials' popularity lies; television brings history to life and makes it *interesting* . . . and easier, too, of course. After all, who'd bother researching so carefully into Henry VIII's life, or Elizabeth I's, or the Strauss family's; and how many people would be tempted to read the whole of *War and Peace?*

The research for such television dramas is a mammoth task, make no mistake about that. Books, paintings and papers are all carefully studied, so that everything is as correct as it possibly could be – and that includes the costumes.

John Bloomfield, the Costume Designer for *The Six Wives of Henry VIII*, worked for almost a year on the series.

No doubt who this costume belonged to, and in his larger days, too! In the television series Henry VIII wore this during the time of Catherine Howard. Oh, and that's Will Somers's, the jester's costume in the background.

Henry plus wives – in costume at least.

A research sample for the series of Elizabeth R.

He spent three months doing basic preparations at the National Portrait Gallery, Windsor Castle and various libraries, going through all the books, papers and paintings that he could lay his hands on – paying special attention to the drawings by Holbein.

Such intensive background research is very useful to a Costume Designer because it means that he gets the feel of the period in history and knows exactly the sort of clothes which are suitable without having to refer back to pictures all the time.

Of course when John Bloomfield was designing the costumes for *The Six Wives of Henry VIII* there were more difficulties than usual because

Another of Elizabeth's costumes. This one is an exact copy of the "Ditchley" portrait of Elizabeth I, painted by Marcus Gheeraerts the Younger in 1592.

A vivacious costume for a vivacious Queen; can you guess which one? Anne Boleyn, of course, and the other costume belonged to one of her ladies-in-waiting.

of the changes in fashion over the period and the influence of fashions from abroad, due to the number and variation in his choice of wives, two of whom came from the continent. But the difficulties didn't end even here, for each costume had to relate to all the others in the scenes and, of course, they all had to blend in with the backgrounds.

Because of the large cast it was decided to make things simpler by dressing each of the various families portrayed in shades of one colour, i.e. greens for the Seymours and reds for the Howards. In this way the colour schemes were more easily kept under control and it helped the viewer to remember who was who!

FROM DESIGN TO GARMENT

Finally, the designs are ready, planned with sets and actors and actresses in mind. Three hundred in all, including twenty-five for Keith Michell, the actor who played Henry VIII. Now the problem remains to make them all economically, and yet so that they look as rich and sumptuous as any original court dress would have been.

The first difficulty is that they just don't make the same sort of materials any more, things like Italian Renaissance cut velvet just don't exist. And so the 'richness' had to be created on cheaper materials. Furnishing fabrics came into their own, at least they were the right weight, and they were painted, using screen printing methods. Fabric patterns with an embossed

effect were achieved by painting the original material with fibre pens and then painting over.

Such a large job couldn't be undertaken by one person, so John Bloomfield gathered together a team of experts, including cutters, dressmakers, artworkers, a furrier, and two assistants from the Costume Department, who proved to have hidden talents as jewellery makers, milliners and shoemakers. The 'jewellery', by the way, was mostly ironmongery bric-a-brac, sprayed with gold paint!

Henry VIII's costume proved to be a problem too, as the series covered the King's life from being a slim young man to being an enormous old one. Of course, Keith Michell had to wear a good deal of heavy padding when he played the old Henry VIII, and this meant it took between thirty and forty-five minutes to get on all the special padding, the special underwear *and* the special tights!

ELIZABETHAN WEAR

But *The Six Wives of Henry VIII* hasn't been the only historical drama to present a mammoth task for its Costume Designer. Elizabeth Waller was faced with similar problems when she was asked to design the costumes for *Elizabeth R*. She had to produce the styles and the lavishness of the Elizabethan court within the framework of a budget, a time limit, modern methods and the director's visual requirements. Not an easy task, I think you'll agree! Especially when you realise how much styles, in both size and decoration, altered during Elizabeth's reign.

As was the case with Henry VIII, a good deal of research was done into the life and times of Elizabeth I, so that the picture presented was as near the original as possible. The design work was based upon contemporary portraits and descriptions of the period, and some of the designs were fully worked out colour sketches, while others were just quick pencil sketches of the line, or the material, or the decoration. Some were changed later, of course, perhaps a different colour or a different sort of trimming; but the period was always strictly adhered to.

In all twenty-five costumes were made for Elizabeth I, played by Glenda Jackson, and fifty-seven for the other principal actors. Most of the costumes were made outside the BBC, and all Glenda Jackson's costumes were

made by one woman, Mrs Jean Hunnisett. Elaborate embroidery was added to the costumes by Mrs Phyllis Thorold.

The dominating influence on clothes of the Elizabethan period was Spanish, so the clothes were rigid and concealing and the women were encased in rigid corsets and cage-like petticoats, called Spanish farthingales. However the Queen's own influence on fashion was enormous and this is shown in the 'anglicisation' of a good many of the fashions; somehow she managed to get the rigid Spanish lines softened a little, especially later in the reign when the Spanish fashion supremacy gave way to the French. During the last years of the Queen's reign the huge French farthingales and equally enormous starched ruffs became very fashionable, and it is, perhaps, in such outfits that Elizabeth I is best remembered.

FANCY THE JOB?

But back to the present day and a little up-to-date information for those of you who might be interested in becoming part of this hard-working but exciting world behind the scenes.

Well, let's talk about the theatre, because there are probably more openings there than there are in television, especially for beginners. You'd probably like a job that combines your interest in fashion with your interest in the theatre, and that means a job in 'wardrobe', with the hope of one day becoming a wardrobe mistress', a job which usually means maintaining the costumes and seeing to the making of clothes for a specific production.

There are several different ways of getting into 'wardrobe', it's probably better for *you* to decide which method you'll be most successful at!

Nowadays more and more young people are doing art school diploma courses, having decided that they'll probably get further with qualifications, which is probably true. Such courses are for Theatre Design, and they include costume design and cutting. Or you can do a shorter two-year wardrobe course, but with a Theatre Design course you're likely to find a greater scope for jobs later on.

You can, if you like, take a fashion course at college; this will give you a good grounding on cutting and sewing which will certainly be useful later on. Or you can start at the bottom and

work your way up. Big theatre costumiers, like Nathan or Berman in London, usually take on apprentices if they show some flair.

However some girls have actually started in the theatre itself, starting out as dressers under the eagle eye of the wardrobe mistress, and picking up all the tricks of the trade as they went along. But make no mistake about it, if you start out this way you're definitely starting out at the bottom. You'll be picking up bits of discarded clothing, helping to dress the actors, and running here, there and everywhere; but you can work your way up . . . up to a point. As with most jobs nowadays, qualifications tend to count for a little more than experience, and if you choose to enter the profession this way you might find that your progress is limited.

But if you can see yourself, eventually, as choosing and buying clothes, finding materials and making up clothes, and researching period looks when you're working with a designer like John Bloomfield or Elizabeth Waller, then this is the sort of job for you. Remember, however, that the big jobs are usually freelance, so don't count on security, and the hours can be long and demanding. So, apart from talent, you're going to need a lot of energy, an adaptable personality and a real love of the job.

And if you've got all these, perhaps we'll be seeing some of your handiwork on television one of these days. . . .

A beautiful costume for a less than beautiful queen! This one was worn by the German Anne of Cleves in the series. And that's another of Keith Michell's costumes in the background.

One of the costumes designed by Elizabeth Waller and made by Jean Hunnisett for Glenda Jackson. This costume is an exact copy of the "Armada" portrait of Elizabeth I, dated 1588 and attributed to George Gower.

SEWit andSEE

says Glynis Holland

Do you sometimes find that you just can't keep up with the speed at which fashions change these days? Often by the time you've saved up enough to buy that outfit you saw in the magazine it's disappeared completely from the fashion scene.

So what's the solution? Easy. Sew it yourself!

Sewing your own clothes saves you money, and it also means that you can be first with the latest styles. And if you need any more persuading, think of all those times you've seen a really super outfit, but thought, "If only it had long sleeves" or "If only the waist was more fitted".

Well, when you make things yourself you can adapt all the basic fashion shapes and styles until they're just right for *you*.

Here are three ideas for outfits to sew yourself. They're all made from McCall's patterns, which you can buy in most large stores.

Choose your pattern, choose your fabric, set yourself aside a few spare evenings — and away you go. Sew it and see!

This super trendy outfit is from McCall's pattern UK40, and it's a stunning style for chilly days. Choose a fairly thick, but not stiff, fabric for the jacket, and one which hangs well for the wide pants. Our model's outfit shows one of fashion's all time great ideas — a combination of plain and patterned fabrics. Both jacket and pants in that check material might be a little overpowering, and both of them in plain grey might have been dull. But check plus plain — equals — great!

After those sporty trousers, take a look at this very feminine, very pretty dress, which would be just right for parties or the disco scene. It's made from McCall's pattern UK36, the skirt buttons up the back, and you can make it with or without those sleeve flounces. It's a pinafore dress, so it is quite versatile, as you can wear a variety of tops underneath. A lovely swingalong dress, which will make sure you're the girl who stands out from the crowd — even in the trendiest disco in town!

Here's one school uniform everyone would love to wear! The gymslip makes a dramatic comeback to the fashion scene — and this photo shows just how super it can look, teamed up with a pretty jumper or blouse, and some fun accessories. Make one of these gymslips from McCall's pattern UK52, take some careful thought about what you're going to wear with it, and how to accessorise — and you'll have yourself a pretty stunning outfit!

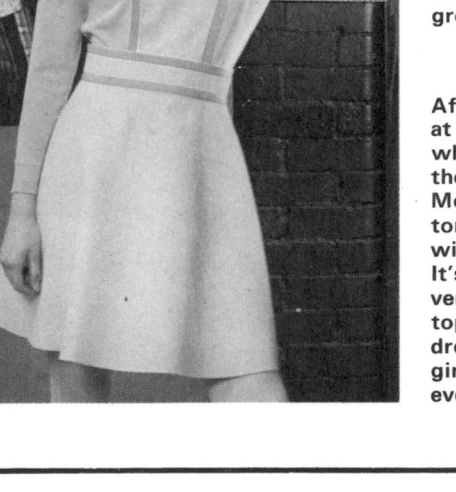

McCall's patterns are available from all main stores in Great Britain and Australia, or direct from: The McCall Pattern Co. Ltd., P.O. Box 27, Cottage Street, Macclesfield, SK11 8EA. For Australian readers, the patterns are available from McCall's Patterns PTY Ltd., 17/25 Spring Street, Bondi Junction, New South Wales, 2022, Australia.

Preserved for Posterity

Gudrun Heatley visits the permanent home of the famous and infamous.

What's the first name that springs to mind when you think of waxworks? Madame Tussaud? Yes, I think it's probably the first name that everyone thinks of, she must be one of the most famous show women in the world. And her fame has lasted quite some time.

Born in 1761, Madame Tussaud — or Marie Grosholtz as she was then known — left her birthplace at the age of six to live with her German-Swiss uncle, Dr. Curtius. He was the man who was to introduce her to the world of wax models. In 1770, three years after Marie's arrival, Dr. Curtius opened his exhibition of life-size wax figures.

Marie must have been fascinated right from the beginning, for she entered into the spirit of wax modelling at a very early age, making a large number of figures. Her most famous from that time — which survives to this day and remains in the exhibition — was of one of France's greatest writers, Voltaire. This wax portrait was done when she was only seventeen.

Wax modelling at that time was very fashionable and Marie spent several years at Versailles teaching the King's younger sister the art. During this time. Dr. Curtius was taking advantage of the popularity of waxworks and

The first portraits of Louis XVI and Marie Antoinette were exhibited by Dr. Curtius, the Queen's dress coming from her own dressmaker, a Mademoiselle Bertin. The Royal Family sat again for Madame Tussaud in 1790.

enlarged his exhibitions on the Boulevard du Temple and the Palais Royal.

But the rumbles of revolution were to be heard in Paris and when the Bastille was stormed, Dr. Curtius was among the leaders, with his niece by his side. When the governor was murdered in the Bastille, Marie and her uncle were ready to make his death mask. And so, throughout the revolution that followed, Marie helped her uncle make the death masks of a great number of the famous people who lost their heads at the guillotine. This must have been a nerve-wracking task for Marie, for among these victims were some of the people she'd grown to know and love.

After an unhappy marriage, Marie, now known as Madame Tussaud, left France for England, bringing with her the eldest of her two sons and also the exhibition that she'd inherited after Curtius's death. Monsieur Tussaud was left in charge of the Paris exhibition, which he mortgaged to balance his gambling debts, and then lost altogether in 1847. By this time Madame Tussaud's other two children had travelled to England to join her, and from that time on she neither saw nor wrote to her husband again.

Madame Tussaud's aim in coming to England was to take her waxworks exhibition on tour and for thirty-three

That famous lady herself . . . I'll bet Madame Tussaud never dreamt that her exhibition would one day contain the likenesses of the first men on the moon.

No need to tell you who this is! He stands resplendent in the Exhibition, for once in harmony with all of his six wives. . . .

Mary Stuart in her last moments. Anything more gruesome than this scene has its place in the Chamber of Horrors.

years this is exactly what she did, visiting schools, setting up her models in assembly rooms, town halls and theatres. The models were displayed against baize backcloths and festoons and illuminated to make them look as life-like as possible.

But at the age of 74 travelling was becoming a little tiresome for Madame Tussaud and so she decided to install her travelling exhibition in permanent premises. Baker Street was decided upon as the best site because it was so close to a new innovation—the Railways.

Madame Tussuad seemed tireless. Each day found her sitting at her customary table at the entrance to the Exhibition, greeting old friends and new, and this custom was to continue almost to the year of her death. She continued modelling, too, until the grand age of 81.

By the time Madame Tussaud died, in 1850, the Exhibition was very definitely established, a firm foundation for Madame Tussaud's as it is today.

FAMOUS FACES

There's something very disturbing about coming face to face with the exact images of people you've only seen in newspapers or on television. At first you feel quite a shock when you gaze up at Tom Jones, or Steve McQueen, or even Henry VIII!

But how about a stop in The Grand Hall first? Meet the Queen and her family, see past politicians side-by-side with present politicians, and famous statesman like Sir Winston Churchill and John Kennedy.

A peep inside Buckingham Palace, and some members of the Royal Family are at home!

One of the most fascinating experiences of the whole of Madame Tussaud's Exhibition is to live through The Battle of Trafalgar. Through the gunshots come the strains of *Heart of Oak*, the tune that the bands were playing as Nelson's ships approached the French and Spanish. And finally, after the flashes of gunfire, the smoke of the gunpowder, the creaking of the wooden ships, and the smell of sea, stockholm tar and hemp rope, the visitor comes to the final scene. Nelson is dead, but even in death the victory is his and the bells peal mournfully for his death and joyously for his final success.

44

George Best, in fine football form from the looks of things.

Enter into the darkness of the 'Heroes-Live' exhibition and there, in splashes of sight and sound you'll see some of the most famous people around today — but watch out for that right!

Or perhaps you'd prefer to take a step back in history and look at the Princes in the Tower, or the Roundheads and the Cavaliers or General de Gaulle, and of course the famous Louis XVI and his family.

But, most people like to look at the present, and that's why Madame Tussaud's has set aside a room full of present-day heroes, including the first men on the moon, Twiggy, George Best, Cilla Black — all complete with special sighting and sound effects to really set the mood.

But even after visiting all these places your Tussaud visit would be incomplete without a special detour for . . . *THE HOUSE OF HORRORS*! Murderers enacting their crimes, and

person, without turning it into a caricature, of course. This is why one of the first stages is the sculpturing of the person's head in clay. Every detail of bone structure has to be noted, for once the likeness is complete, this sculpture is used to make the mould from which the wax castings are taken. These moulds are kept even when a person's appearance changes or if his wax double is removed from the exhibition. In all, ten moulds are kept for every wax casting, so preserving a permanent record.

Building the body isn't an easy task either. This plaster torso must somehow convey the identity of the

It's Steve McQueen!

victims suffering over and over again. But don't go in if you're of a nervous disposition. . . .

BEHIND THE SCENES

A visit behind the scenes at Madame Tussaud's is just as fascinating as the view that usually greets the visitors, and it is only when you are given a chance to see the backstage work, that you realise just how much patience and skill goes into the wax figures.

Once a person has been chosen as a model, and has agreed to be preserved for posterity, a team of measurers and matchers are put to work. Photographs from every angle, sculptures, measurements, colour-matching — nothing escapes the eagle eye of the Madame Tussaud craftsmen.

And it isn't easy. Features must be easily recognisable and yet put forward some of the character of the

person as much as the head does, and yet still look 'human' when dressed. And, of course, every measurement must be exact.

Once the body is complete, the chosen wax cast of the head is finished. Everything has to be perfectly correct: skin, lips, eyes, teeth, hair . . . every detail is faithfully reproduced. The wax is worked with colour and brush, kept transparent or made opaque depending on the person's skin texture. The hair is cut into the scalp strand by strand, so that it falls in exactly the right way and, of course, the texture and colour are perfectly matched. Every beauty device is used so that the model looks completely realistic; can you imagine George Best with *false* eyelashes?

Finally, when legs, arms, body and head meet for the first time, it is the turn of the dressmaker or tailor to add his or her talent to this Madame

Well, this is probably the nearest you'll ever get to seeing Tom Jones performing live!

waxwork and after the oil painting had been used to get a better likeness, it was hung in the Exhibition Hall, where it still hangs today.

Perhaps one of the nicest things about Madame Tussaud's is the interest that the sitter's take in their own models. They do their utmost to see that their double looks as authentic as possible. For this reason Queen Juliana of the Netherlands presented one of her evening dresses to dress her model in, and Lord Montgomery went to great pains to point out that a medal ribbon was missing from his uniform. In the case of Prime Minister Yoshida of Japan, his daughter arranged the model's clothes with the ritual intricacy that only she knew.

But things don't always happen this way; Madame Tussaud's have been known to make donations of

their own, as in the case of the clothes that are on display at Chartwell, the late Sir Winston Churchill's home. The Garter robes to be seen there are the ones made by Tussaud's wardrobes for Churchill's wax model.

And so, with the model dressed, it is complete. Only a place has to be found for it. Will it go next to Queen Victoria and her party, or the famous Sleeping Beauty, or is it more likely to be placed next to Tom Jones. . . . why not go and see for yourself?

Take a step into outer space and then one more step and you're on the moon. . . .

Tussaud special. The clothes have to be chosen and made, and then the model has to be dressed. Each garment must fold, flow, and crease just as it would if it were being worn by a real person. Historical costumes are followed down to the last detail.

During the war when all sorts of materials and clothing were in short supply Madame Tussaud's still managed to flourish, thanks to some of their famous sitters. President Truman's suit was brought over from the White House by Prime Minister Attlee, so that the President's wax double would look as realistic as possible. But even before the Second World War, in 1870 to be exact, Madame Tussaud's were receiving unexpected help from outside. . . . A mysterious packing case arrived from St. Petersburgh, without any letter, and containing a uniform and an oil painting. After three months, the mystery was finally solved — a Prince Troubetzki called in at the exhibition to say that Popoff, the Minister of Police, had reported to the Russian Czar how poor the likeness of Nicholas the First was. Of course, the matter was rectified. The uniform was used to dress the new

Cilla Black, against a backcloth of memories.

And, while you're there, give a thought to some of the models who haven't been treated as well as the ones before you. . . . The poor old Duke of Orleans was pelted with rotten eggs in 1793. Sir Winston Churchill had his head shattered in 1954. Lord Snowdon was carried off to a North London telephone box in 1960, President Tito was left outside the Yugoslavian Embassy in 1965, and in the same year somebody gave Harold Wilson a trip to Manchester!

Still, it just goes to show how realistic they look . . . they treat them as they'd like to treat their human counterparts.

It's time to dye

This is dyeing with a difference. It's called 'Tie and Dye' and clothes dyed like this are usually expensive. But you can dye it yourself with Dylon Cold, Multi-purpose or Liquid Dyes — the type depends on the fabric you're going to dye, and they're available from department stores and hardware shops. It's quite simple, just follow the instructions on the container.

Your design depends on the kind of tying that you do. Here are a few suggestions.

For the effect on Colour Picture 1 mark out the pattern with a pencil or chalk first and then knot where you want the rings to appear. Tie the knots very tightly.

Knotting again, but in a sequence this time. Colour Picture 2.

Tie in a stone and butter beans for this pattern of circles. Or experiment with corks, coins, dried peas and shells. Colour Picture 3.

To get this marbling effect, crumple up the fabric in your hand and then bind tightly with thread or elastic bands. Crumple in different places for each colour that you use. Colour Picture 4.

Clump-tying again. This time a larger stone has been tied in. This 'lump' has been criss-crossed with thread and the fabric has also been bound at intervals. Colour Picture 5.

Needle and thread instead of binding this time. Stitch in the pattern that you want and then pull the thread up tight. Bind round the stitching to be extra sure of the fabric staying in place. Colour Picture 6.

For localised patterns like the ones on this seersucker trouser suit put the parts that aren't to be touched in polythene bags to protect them from the dye. Colour Picture 7.

1 **2**

 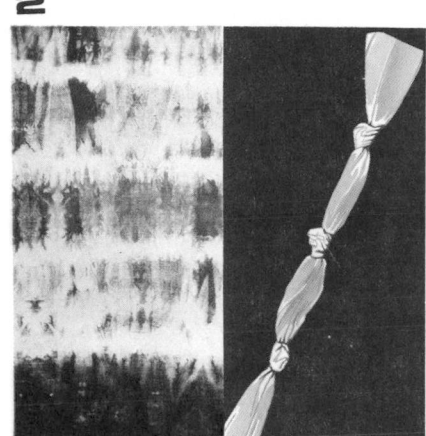

3 **4**

 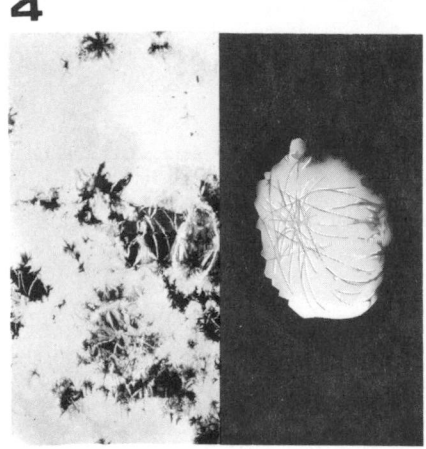

5 **6**

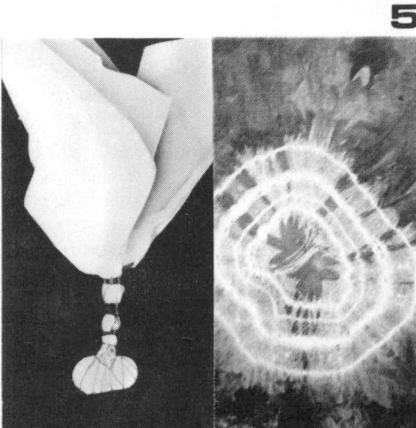 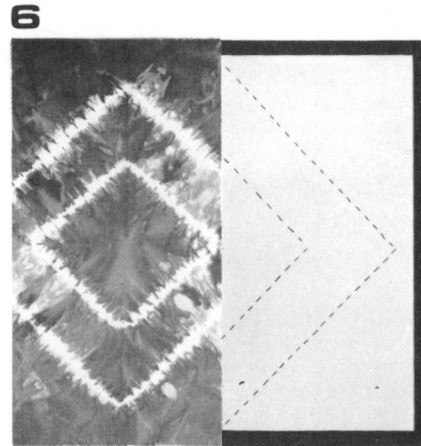

7

Set against the world famous Sydney Harbour Bridge, the Opera House is now the city's most spectacular and controversial landmark.

SYDNEY OPERA HOUSE

The unique shell-like roof of the Opera House presented many constructional problems, which a computer had to solve before work could commence.

The curtains of the drama theatre have an abstract design with a moon theme and were woven from Australian wool in the 500-year-old French Chateau Felletin at Aubusson.

48

Already Australia's most controversial and spectacular building, when the Sydney Opera House was finally completed in 1973 it was a triumph of construction and engineering skills, blending 17th century craftsmanship with 20th century technology, and turning the design sketches of Jørn Utzon into a spectacular reality.

AN ARCHITECTURAL DREAM

When Danish architect Jørn Utzon won an international competition in 1957 with his sail-like structures, nobody thought that it would take so long to make this dream a reality.

The site chosen for the Opera House was on the shores of Sydney Harbour on Bennelong Point. Mr. Utzon himself supervised the first stage of construction, and the base podium and concourse was completed in 1962.

Later, due to a disagreement, Mr. Utzon resigned, and a consortium of Australian architects took over the project.

THE JIGSAW CEILING

The ceiling of the Concert Hall hangs from the spheroid shell roofs, with the main planes flowing freely and without corners. The ceiling caused many constructional problems, which were finally resolved with the aid of a computer. The ceiling was fitted together like a giant jigsaw in which some 70,000 square feet of white birch veneer was made up into 1,750 panels with more than 50,000 dimensions and curves.

THE PIPE ORGAN

When it is completed in 1974, the pipe organ in the Opera House will be the largest mechanical pipe organ in the world.

Designed by Ron Sharp, a self-taught organmaker, the organ will have 9,600 pipes. The largest visible pipe is about 30 feet high with a 17 inch diameter and is made of pure tin. The smallest pipe is the size of a pencil with a resonating end about a quarter of an inch long.

The massive organ will also have a closed television monitor on the console so that the organist can see the conductor on the platform some thirty feet below. It will also have a wash-basin just outside the loft so that organists and tuners may wash their hands.

THE HOME OF THE ARTS

The Sydney Opera House will provide a superb setting for the arts, and a conference centre, and already it is a famous landmark of unique design.

It will contain a Concert Hall, an Opera Theatre, a Drama Theatre, a Chamber-Music-Cinema Hall, a Rehearsal-Recording Studio and a Reception-Recital Studio.

There will also be a first-class restaurant with magnificent harbour views, and another popular restaurant under a separate shell roof with additional outdoor seating.

The halls and theatres will provide facilities for symphony concerts, opera, ballet, drama, chamber music, musicals, jazz concerts, film festivals and radio and television broadcasts.

Tapestry curtains for the opera and drama theatres were designed by Australian artist John Coburn. The tapestries are made from Australian wool and are fireproof. The opera theatre curtains have a sun theme and pure gold thread has been used, while the drama theatre curtains are in cool blues and greens echoing a moon theme.

In anticipation of the Opera House being used for international conferences and receptions, both the concert hall and the opera theatre will each be equipped to handle five simultaneous language translations, while the drama theatre, the chamber music hall and a major rehearsal area will each handle three translations.

The waters of Sydney Harbour lap three sides of the Opera House site at Bennelong Point. The point is named after an aborigine befriended by Governor Phillip, founder of the first Australian settlement.

The world's biggest mechanical action organ pipe built by Ron Sharp in the Concert Hall of the Opera House has 9,600 pipes and 113 stops.

The Tale of
BEATRIX POTTER

In the summer of 1866 a baby girl was born to the Potters of Bolton Gardens. Nothing changed very much; a third floor room became a nursery, a nurse was employed, but Mr. Potter continued to spend a good deal of his time at one or other of his clubs, and Mrs. Potter continued her departures by coach every afternoon at two, to go calling. Indeed, Helen Beatrix Potter was almost non-existent as far as her family were concerned.

Childhood was lonely for Beatrix, as it was for most children born into similar well-to-do homes in Victorian times. Her parents were upper middle class, which meant that they weren't society, but her father didn't have to work and their home was as comfortable as Mrs. Potter allowed it to be. Beatrix remained in her nursery most of the time, only being allowed out for regular afternoon walks with her nurse and occasionally seeing her parents when they sent for her.

Certainly nothing was done to make Beatrix's childhood a very interesting one; indeed, Mr. and Mrs. Potter would have thought it very strange even to consider whether their daughter's life was interesting or not. She had a black wooden doll to play with and a rather grubby white flannelette pig whenever she visited her grandmother's, and it must be admitted that Beatrix was quite happy.

It was on such visits to her grandmother's that Beatrix began to realize how fascinating was life outside the four walls of Bolton Gardens. She would sit for hours under the library table, absorbing the interesting tales that her grandmother loved to tell. As she grew older, however, Beatrix could no longer hide beneath the fringed cloth of the library table, at least not without seeming a little strange, and so she sat opposite her grandmother, pretending to draw butterflies, while she recorded all the interesting snippets of conversation in a code of her own invention.

When Bertram, her brother, was born, life for Beatrix became a little more interesting, especially as he shared her love of drawing and painting when he was old enough. On their long family holidays in Scotland, Beatrix and her brother would spend hours collecting flowers to press and sketching picturesque cottages and unusual fungi; they even brought home dead animals! These they would skin, or if they were past skinning they would boil the carcass until only the bones remained. On one such holiday they discovered a dead fox, which they sneaked back to their holiday home, where they boiled it and reassembled its skeleton so that they could draw it —and they somehow managed to keep the whole thing a secret!

Unlike Beatrix, however, Bertram had to go to school, but after their long Scottish holidays she was never quite as lonely. She would spend hours drawing and painting the pressed flowers that they'd brought home between large sheets of blotting paper, or sketching the skeletons of the fieldmice which they'd somehow managed to sneak into their luggage! The nursery even housed a family of snails that Beatrix tended with great care, and who seemed more than happy with their plant-pot home.

It wasn't long before the nursery at Bolton Gardens began to look like a zoo. Shy and tongue-tied even with relatives, Beatrix was a different person when surrounded by her pets. Two wild mice lived like lords on milk and cracker crumbs; a rabbit whose home was supposed to be a hutch in the back garden spent most of his time stretched out on the rug in front of the fire, and in a parrot's cage in the corner two bats hung upside down, flying round the room at twilight and resting on Beatrix's fingers for a few moments before orbiting again. And, finally, there was Tiggy, a hedgehog who liked nothing better than to drink her milk from a doll's teacup.

But childhood was slipping by quickly and eventually Miss Hammond, Beatrix's governess, left, to be replaced by two younger women, one of whom was to teach French and the other German. But it was Miss Carter, the German teacher, who was to hold the key to Beatrix Potter's literary success, although nobody was aware of this at the time. . . .

Beatrix was never strong and she suffered a great deal from rheumatic pains which left her very weak, and during one particularly bad bout her long hair, which reached her knees, had to be cropped short because so much of it was falling out. But nothing could prevent her drawing, especially when she became so interested in fungi. She would spend hours staring into Bertram's microscope and drawing various samples of fungus. Painstakingly, she would record every tiny fibre that was visible and every variation in colour.

Over the years Beatrix's collection of botanical drawings grew, until she was quite sure that she had enough for a book. The idea of a book also seemed to appeal to Beatrix's uncle, Sir Henry Roscoe, for he offered to take her to Kew where she could meet some of the most eminent botanists of the day. But all was to no avail: either her drawings were too pretty or the notes which she'd added herself were ridiculously amateurish, or so the learned gentlemen said. For a time Beatrix continued drawing her fungi despite her disappointment, but eventually her portfolios were laid aside to gather dust.

But Beatrix didn't give up painting altogether. She turned instead to novel animal scenes, rabbit families to decorate the nursery walls of her nieces and nephews, and working models of furnished mouse holes and rabbit's greengrocery shops.

When Miss Carter, Beatrix's German governess, left to get married, Beatrix was left alone once more. For company she kept a couple of lizards in a box and she learnt Shakespeare's plays by heart. Even when she travelled, her pets weren't far away. Her plain clothes, stout boots, sensible umbrella and travelling rabbit hutch often caused stares when she waited on station platforms while accompanying her parents on one of their many visiting trips around the country.

Occasionally, Beatrix did manage to slip away from her demanding mother and father, and on such occasions she often visited her now-married governess, who had a rapidly growing family. The children delighted Beatrix, and she delighted them with her animal stories and lightning sketches of the characters.

When Noel, one of the children fell ill and Beatrix had to travel a great deal with her parents, she began to write him letters, charmingly illustrated. And when she hadn't any news to write, she would write a story instead, with beautiful illustrations. Noel was delighted, as were the many other children who received similar treats over the years.

It was these letters to Noel which gave Beatrix her ideas for her first book, *The Tale of Peter Rabbit*. Unfortunately for them, a number of publishers turned down Beatrix's manuscript and illustrations, but this time she wasn't giving up so easily. She decided to publish the book herself, privately.

The book was a great success and Beatrix sold all the copies to various relatives and friends, some of whom viewed the venture with a little amusement. This time when Beatrix Potter offered her book to a publishers they listened, and it wasn't long before Frederick Warne & Company published the second edition of *Peter Rabbit,* this time in colour.

The book was a sell-out and Warne's were soon clamouring for more of Beatrix Potter's work, and so *Squirrel Nutkin, Benjamin Bunny, Mrs Twiggy-Winkle, Jemima Puddle-Duck* and lots more began to roll off the presses. Their popularity and fame stretched to the continent and over the Atlantic to America. Models of the most popular of the animals appeared in toyshops everywhere, most of which distressed Beatrix because they were so badly designed and made.

Despite her success in the literary field and the fact that Beatrix was more than old enough to look after herself, her parents were very possessive and rarely allowed her out on her own. On one occasion she was invited to stay at her cousin's home, Caroline Hutton who lived in Gloucester, a trip that her parents viewed with disapproval. Eventually, however, she was grudgingly allowed to go. The visit proved to be a great success because it was here that Beatrix first heard the tale of *The Tailor of Gloucester*, about which she wrote and illustrated a book

Beatrix's literary success led her to meet more people than she'd ever met in her life before, including the Warne family whose publishing company produced her books. And although she was still very shy, she wasn't quite as tongue-tied now, and quite frequently she could be seen chatting to one or other of the Warnes when she visited their home in Bedford Square. It was quite unlike her own home, it was light and bright and filled with children and laughter, and Beatrix loved it.

It was here that she began to love Norman Warne too. He was a kind, good-hearted man with a happy nature that made everyone like him. Like Norman's sister Millie, who was to become one of Beatrix's best friends, Beatrix was shy and so the friendly publisher took her under his wing. They were both about the same age, nearing forty, and they had a great many interests in common, and in the summer of 1905 Norman proposed and Beatrix accepted, despite her parents' complete opposition.

At last Beatrix was truly happy, although at times things were very difficult because of her parents' attitude. She spent a good deal of her time at Bedford Square, telling stories to the various Warne nieces and nephews, and becoming great friends with Millie.

Then, as the summer was drawing to a close, disaster struck. Norman Warne became ill and died. Normally robust and healthy he became sickly and pale, and it was discovered that he was in the final stages of leukaemia. By the end of August, Beatrix was alone once more.

Grief-stricken, Beatrix decided that she had to get away, and so she took the biggest step of her life. She became the owner of Hill Top Farm in the Lake District.

The Lake District, with its picturesque farms, villages and shops gave Beatrix Potter a good deal of inspiration for her books, and finally she also found happiness and marriage there. She became Mrs. Heelis of Castle Cottage, the wife of a local solicitor, again much to her parents' displeasure.

The farm needed a great deal doing to it and Beatrix threw herself into the task wholeheartedly. Although sometimes the term 'wholeheartedly' could have been taken a little too literally. Especially when she nearly fell through the kitchen ceiling from the room above, much to the concern of the men who were working in the kitchen at the time!

It would seem that being a wife and farmer left Beatrix very little time, for she wrote little after her second marriage, concentrating on her sheep farming and on efforts to preserve parts of her beloved Lake District. A good many of the pieces of National Trust land in the Lake District were donated by Beatrix Potter.

Beatrix Potter died on the 22nd December 1943 at the age of seventy-seven years, as quietly and unobtrusively as she had lived, leaving a heritage of stories to children all over the world.

The Milky Way

Not all peoples of the world get their milk from a cow. Some of them drink the milk from goats, or reindeer, sheep, camels, or even horses! But wherever it comes from, milk is one of the best foods you can get. It contains so much goodness that it would almost be possible for you to live on milk alone, without eating any other foods at all — in fact most babies do thrive on milk alone for the first few weeks of their lives, so milk has to be good.

In days gone by the dairyman led his cows up to the town dweller's door and milked one of them on the doorstep so there was just enough milk to give to one household. Housewives then really knew the milk was fresh! Later the milk cart was loaded with churns full of fresh milk which was ladled out into the housewife's own jug, and nowadays the milk comes from the dairy where it has been purified and packed in sterile bottles or cartons. It is delivered to your door as fresh and clean as if the cow had been milked on the doorstep!

But you may think that milk is rather boring to drink on its own, so there are some super recipes using milk and cream to whip up the most exciting supper savouries and delicious sweets.

A Milky Breakfast

Hot Breakfast Quickie
1 Make up instant porridge according to the instructions.
2 Add honey or sugar to taste.
— and try these for a delicious change —
— add the juice from an orange and some chopped dates.
— or a sliced banana sprinkled with lemon juice.
— or slices of fresh orange or apple.
— or some fruit yogurt and chopped apple.
— or a little lemon juice and some raisins.

Alpine Breakfast (for 4)
10 heaped tablespoons quick porridge oats
¾ pint milk
1 oz chopped nuts
2 eating apples
1 tablespoon lemon juice
1 oz raisins or sultanas
1–2 ozs caster sugar

Method

1 Put the oats into a bowl and stir in the milk.
2 Add the nuts. Core the apple, chop finely and sprinkle with lemon juice.
3 Add the apple, fruit and sugar to the oats, stir well, and enjoy breakfast the alpine way.

Toasties

Bacon Toasties (for 4)

4 slices bread	2 ozs cheese
butter	2 tablespoons milk
4 sliced tomatoes	4 rashers bacon

Method

1 Toast the bread on both sides. Grill the bacon.
2 Butter toast and cover with slices of tomato.
3 Mix together cheese and milk and spread over tomatoes.
4 Grill until cheese melts and turns golden. Serve topped with bacon rashers.

French Toasties (for 4)

1 egg   *salt and pepper*
¼ pint milk   *butter for frying*
4 slices bread

Method

1 Beat egg, milk and seasoning together in a shallow dish.
2 Heat the butter gently in a frying pan.
3 Dip bread into the egg mixture and fry over a medium heat until golden brown on both sides.
4 Enjoy super French toasties with sausages and tomatoes.

Teatime Treats

Hot Cheese Soup (for 4)

1 oz butter   *1 small onion, chopped*
1 oz flour   *1 pint milk*
½ pint water   *4 ozs Cheddar cheese*
salt and pepper

Method

1 Melt the butter and lightly fry the finely chopped onion. Stir in the flour and cook for a minute.
2 Remove from heat and gradually add milk, water and onion mixture.
3 Return to heat and bring to the boil, stirring.
4 Season and simmer gently for 5 minutes.
5 Remove from heat and stir in the grated cheese.
Serve.

Deep Sea Puffs (for 12)

Oven at Mark 8 or 450°F
13 ozs puff pastry (packet)
1 beaten egg   *1 oz butter*
1 oz flour   *½ pint milk*
4 ozs peeled prawns

Method

1 Roll out pastry to ¼ inch thick. Cut out 12 rounds with a 2½ inch plain cutter.
2 Place on baking sheet and brush with beaten egg. Bake for 10 minutes.
3 Melt butter in a pan to make the sauce, add flour, mix well and cook for 2–3 minutes. Remove pan from heat and gradually add milk.
4 Return to heat and bring to boil, stirring until thickened. Cook for 2–3 minutes.
5 Add prawns and remaining beaten egg.
6 Remove centres half way down from pastry cases.
7 Fill with the prawn mixture and replace the tops.
These are delicious hot or cold.

Bread and Butter Pudding

6 slices buttered white bread   *3 eggs*
2 ozs mixed dried fruit
2 ozs caster sugar   *¾ pint milk*
pinch of mixed spice
Oven at mark 3 or 325°F

Method

1 Cut each slice of bread into four triangles.
2 Arrange in a pie dish with the mixed fruit. Heat milk until almost boiling.
3 Whisk eggs and sugar together until smooth.
4 Gradually add milk, whisking all the time and pour over bread mixture. Sprinkle with mixed spice and leave to stand (to let the mixture blend together) for 30 minutes.
5 Bake for about 1 hour until firm for a delicious traditional sweet.

Apple-Cheese Fritters (for 4)

4 ozs plain flour   *1 egg*
¼ pint milk
1 tablespoon melted butter
2 ozs Cheddar cheese, grated
2 eating apples   *pinch salt*
to fry —
2 ozs butter   *3 tablespoons oil*

Method

1 Sift the flour and salt into a bowl, and beat into a smooth batter with the egg, milk and butter. Add the cheese.
2 Peel and core apples, and cut into slices.
3 Dip each slice into the batter and fry gently on both sides until golden brown.
4 Drain and serve, sprinkled with icing sugar for a crispy and different way to eat apples.

Creamy Concoctions

Milk is marvellous for the everyday meals, but for an extra-special meal-time use cream for a sweet, or savoury dish.

Apple Coleslaw (for 6)
1 small white cabbage   3 apples
2 dessertspoons lemon juice
small carton of double cream
1 tablespoon salad cream
salt, pepper   paprika pepper
2 ozs raisins

Method
1 Shred cabbage finely.
2 Peel, core and dice apples, and sprinkle with lemon juice
3 Blend cream with salad cream and salt and pepper.
4 Blend with cabbage, apples and raisins.
   You can serve this on a bed of lettuce if you wish, or in a bowl so you can help yourself.

Stuffed Green Peppers (for 4)
oven at mark 4 or 350°F
4 green peppers
$\frac{1}{2}$ lb freshly boiled rice ($\frac{1}{4}$ lb when raw)
$\frac{1}{4}$ lb Lancashire cheese – crumbled
$\frac{1}{4}$ teaspoon mustard
1 small carton cream

5 tablespoons cold water
1 oz butter   salt and pepper

Method
1 Cut the tops off peppers and remove seeds and fibres.
2 Place in a saucepan. Cover with boiling water and simmer for two minutes. Remove and drain.
3 Add the cheese, mustard and cream to the rice, mix and season.
4 Stand peppers in a shallow, heat-proof dish. Fill them with the rice mixture and pour water into the dish.
5 Place a knob of butter on each pepper.
6 Cook for 15 minutes.
   Serve these as a different vegetable, or on their own at suppertime.

Apple Surprise (for 4)
8 ozs porridge oats
3 ozs brown sugar   2 ozs butter
1 oz plain chocolate, grated
little lemon juice   sugar to taste
small carton double cream

Method
1 Mix the porridge oats and brown sugar and fry in butter until crisp.
2 Peel and core the apples and cook in a little water with lemon juice and sugar to taste.
3 Put alternate layers of crumb mixture and apple into a serving dish, finishing with a layer of crumbs.
4 When quite cold, top with whipped cream and sprinkle with grated chocolate. A tasty sweet for summer or winter.

Coffee Cream Ice (for 4)
Once you have made real ice cream at home you'll never enjoy a bought ice cream quite so much again. To make this favourite sweet you need –
2 eggs, separated   2 ozs icing sugar
3 tablespoons coffee essence (liquid)
small carton double cream

Method
1 Whisk the egg whites until very stiff, and then whisk in the icing sugar.
2 Whisk the egg yolks and coffee essence and whisk gradually into the egg whites.
3 Lightly whip the cream and fold into the coffee mixture.
4 Pour into an ice tray or shallow tin and freeze it in the freezer part of the fridge.
You don't need to whisk the ice cream again – just serve with a wafer and enjoy it.

These recipes prove that you don't have to eat food that is dull to keep healthy. So keep fit the milky way.

LET'S TRY LEATHERWORK

Leatherwork as a hobby is not only a fascinating pastime, but also a very useful one. Just think how cheaply you can keep up to date, fashionwise, if you can make your own leather bags, purses, belts — and even clothes, if you're really ambitious.

But before you rush out to buy a large piece of leather to turn into vast numbers of belts, purses and bags, just stop a moment and think! Hand-made leather things can either be very good to look at and compare favourably with shop bought ones, or they can just look sloppy, and exactly what they are: 'homemade'. The secret lies in planning. The individuality of your leatherwork lies in its design *not* in its workmanship.

I know it is very tempting to start on something large and impressive, which you can show to all your friends, but I think that you'll find that by starting on smaller items your confidence will increase and your enthusiasm will not begin to wane before the article is finished. After all, beginner dressmakers don't usually start by trying to copy a Dior model, do they?

Well, now that we've got the dos and don'ts over with, it's time to start. How about a belt, up-to-the-minute fashionwise, easy to make, and something which will impress your friends too.

Here's where you come into your own. Make it plain or fancy, it's entirely up to you, and the basic shape is the same anyway.

There are a number of points to remember, however, before you begin your belt:

1. Always measure correctly; don't guess.

2. You should have all the materials ready *before* you start, and that includes the buckle. Buy the buckle just a fraction bigger than the finished width of the belt, so that it will fasten neatly.

3. Always make sure that the glue of one step has completely dried before you go on to the next step.

Well, if you've decided on your leather, colour and texture, it's time to go shopping. You will need a strip of leather, the width of your choice, which is long enough to go round your waist and eight inches to spare. Here is the basis of your belt. Buy also a small piece of felt and a buckle of your choice.

If you decide to round off one end of your belt, do this now. But if you prefer a square end then simply fit the buckle into place and then glue back the end of the belt securely, so that the buckle is firmly in place.

Your piece of felt should be the same length and width as your finished belt. Glue into place on the wrong side of the leather. Now all you have to do is try it on and mark with pins the positions for the holes. Punch in the holes and your belt is complete.

If you have a few pieces of leather perhaps you would like to cut out some shapes and stick them onto your plain belt to make it look really original.

Once you've decided whether you really like leatherwork or not, and if you wish to carry on and make more difficult things, you will have to invest in a few tools to help you.

To make the simple purse shown below, and most of the simple things which can be made in leather, these are all that you will need:

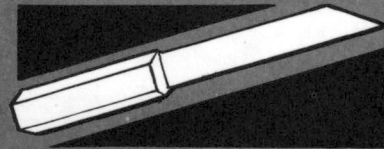

Fig 1:

For your leather work to have a professional appearance it is best to have a sharp knife, like this one, for cutting out, because it will give a neater finish. The one shown here is similar to those used for woodwork and one of these would be most suitable. For thinner leathers, however, you may find that some strong scissors are just as successful.

Fig 2:

The stitching around this purse is called thonging, and for this you will need this special tool which is called a thonging punch. Most handicrafts shops sell them and they are not too expensive.

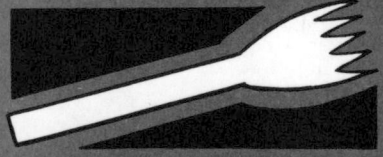

Fig 3:

This piece of equipment, which is called a stitch spacer, is not necessary for our simple purse, but you will find that the majority of leather goods are sewn, and this stitch puncher should prove a good investment.

NOW FOR THE PURSE....

The first thing that you will have to make is a paper pattern, from which you can cut your leather shapes. Using strong brown paper draw inch squares, shown scaled down here, and then carefully draw in the shape of your purse.

When you are perfectly sure that your paper pattern is right and that your purse will be the right shape, cut out the pieces of leather, using your sharp knife. This is best done by fixing the leather to the pattern and then holding it down firmly on a solid surface before you start cutting. Try to use as few strokes of the knife as possible, or you will end up with jagged edges.

Now lay each piece of the purse exactly in its finished position, so that you can punch in the holes for the thonging. But do make sure the pieces are exactly right before you start punching, because one wrong move and your work so far will be wasted. Try practising on odd scraps of leather first.

Measure $\frac{3}{16}$" in from the edges of the leather pieces, put your thonging punch in the correct position, having made sure that your holes will finish in the right place, and then give a light tap with a hammer, this will make three holes. Carry on until you have punched the holes through both sides of the base of the purse and the safety strap, but do not make any holes in the flap at all.

You can buy leather thongs from most handicrafts shops. Now all you have to do is sew the thonging through the holes that you have just made, as shown in the diagram, and your purse is complete. And if you still like leatherwork there are lots of things that you can make now that you have the basic equipment and knowledge ... and just think of all the money you can save by making your own presents!

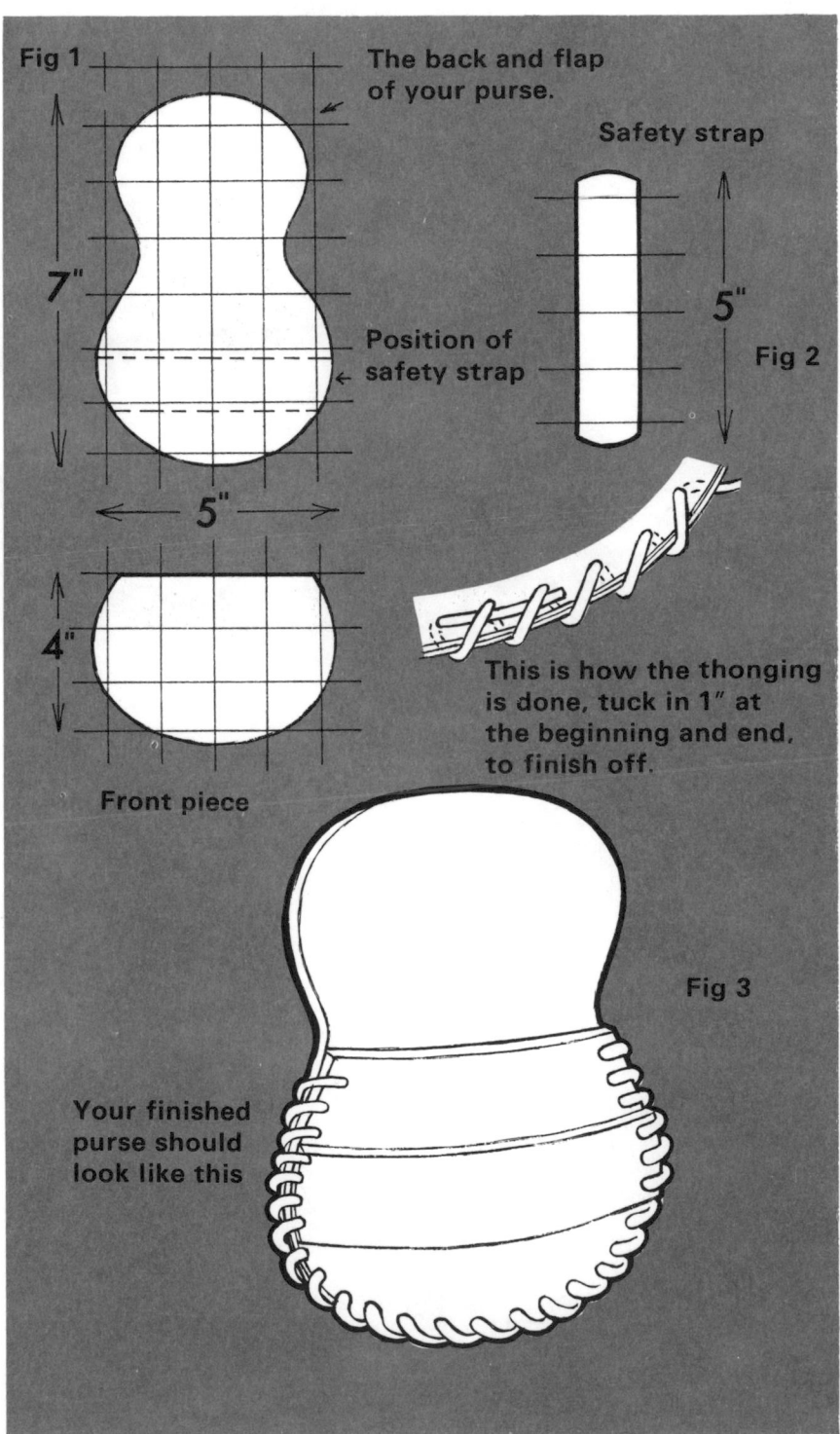

Fig 1

The back and flap of your purse.

Safety strap

7"

Position of safety strap

5"

Fig 2

5"

4"

Front piece

This is how the thonging is done, tuck in 1" at the beginning and end, to finish off.

Fig 3

Your finished purse should look like this

The Rebellion

by Olive L. Groom

Sometime, at some stage of your life, you must face up to change

"I do not understand it in the least," pronounced Aunt Agatha majestically. She was a large lady and the costume of the day, inclining as it did towards voluminous skirts and towering wigs, did nothing to diminish her size. "I cannot feel, my dear Rosalind, that you are at all suited to the fashionable life of London."

"N-no, aunt," Rosalind agreed ruefully. She knew that she was small and rather thin and had dark brown hair instead of beautiful golden curls like Aunt Agatha's daughters; besides, she was shy.

"I daresay Rosalind will be sadly out of place there," prophesied Aunt Amelia, seated stiffly at her niece's other side. "'Tis monstrous unkind of the Earl to insist upon the child's removal to town."

"'Twill be so mortifying for poor Rosalind," sighed Aunt Agatha's eldest daughter with gloomy relish. "How can she hope to know how to conduct herself in an Earl's mansion? Why, I vow the place will be alive with butlers and footmen and abigails by the score. They will all despise our poor cousin, I fear."

Rosalind's pansy-blue eyes sparkled indignantly and she tossed her neat head.

"I am sure I care nothing for what they may think of me," she said, sudden defiance in her soft voice. Then she remembered how truly scared she was of the prospect of living with her aristocratic relatives. "But . . . pray, Aunt, is there no way in which I can escape? *Must* I go away from dear Becky and live in the Earl's house among all those fashionables?"

"Certainly you must, child! You are an heiress and the Earl is your guardian. We should be failing in our duty if we did not send you to take up the station to which Providence has called you," said Aunt Agatha solemnly, clearly thinking poorly of Providence. It would have been so much more to her liking if her own daughter had been an heiress and able to claim the richest Earl in England as her guardian and trustee. Fifteen-year-old Sophia would have enjoyed 'queening it' among all the other well-born, well-to-do young ladies in London instead of languishing here deep in a country village. Rosalind, a year younger than Sophia, was such a quiet little dab of a girl, in Aunt Agatha's opinion; too shy and retiring to make the most of her wealth and the position which would one day be hers.

"Oh dear!" Rosalind herself sighed before, with an obvious effort, she added "Since there seems to be no escape I expect I shall be happy enough when I am grown used to things." Her pretty face brightened.

"At least I shall still have dear old Bunch for my friend."

A combined shriek of horror went up from the two aunts, while Sophia and her younger sisters tittered loudly.

"What a zany you are, cousin," said Sophia pityingly.

"Indeed you will not be allowed to take that animal to London," said Aunt Amelia.

"Heavens, child, a *mongrel* dog in an Earl's mansion! 'Tis quite unheard of; rid your mind of that notion at once," Aunt Agatha demanded trenchantly.

"Then I won't go at all," declared Rosalind spiritedly and the outcry began all over again.

It was not until an hour later that she was able to be alone. Her masterful aunts and cousins had driven away to their own homes on the other side of the village and once more Rosalind was alone with Becky, her former nurse. She had lived in Becky's small cottage ever since the death of her grandfather some six months ago.

Rosalind's parents had died of a fever when she was a baby so that she had been brought up by a succession of housekeepers in her grandfather's home. With his death a distant cousin, the Earl of Allenstone, had been appointed her guardian and

since he had been travelling abroad for some time his young ward had never met him.

Now, it appeared, the Earl was in England again and prepared to open up his stately home for Rosalind, who was fast coming to the opinion that she did not want it.

"I can't go away and leave Bunch. He's always been with me. Becky, my aunts tell me I shall not be permitted to take him to London," Rosalind cried when the visitors were safely gone.

Becky was kind, but not very helpful.

"Now, don't you take on so, dearie. You'll soon settle down in London and forget that rascally dog. You are of the nobility, remember, and you must learn to be a great lady like your dear sainted mother."

"I don't want to be a great lady. I want to stay here with you and Bunch," Rosalind declared in a sudden burst of rebellion before dashing off to her own room.

Here, with brown, shaggy Bunch

curled up blissfully beside her, she sat on the curtain-hung bed and considered the situation. Until a few months ago she had led a carefree if rather lonely life on her grandfather's large country estate. The latter gentleman had been well known for his hasty temper and irritable disposition, and since he had quarrelled violently with all his relations years ago Rosalind had seen her aunts and cousins only on rare occasions.

As she much preferred riding her pony or playing with Bunch to taking tea and making polite conversation Rosalind had not missed her cousins' companionship overmuch, but she had grown shy of meeting strangers.

"I cannot help feeling that Sophia and my aunts are a little put out because I am to go to London, but how I wish I need not. They are quite right, I shall not know how to conduct myself there, and everyone will laugh at me for my country ways and — oh, darling Bunch, I can't bear to leave you." Two large tears rolled down Rosalind's cheeks but she brushed

'Egg-ceedingly Odd.'

Easter, it wouldn't be the same without eggs, would it? Chocolate ones, sugar-coated ones, even hard-boiled ones, gaily decorated. But for some people Easter may never have been quite the same again — after they'd received these eggs. . . .

It would seem that an Easter egg is the next best thing to a valentine, and that's certainly true for a certain girl from France. Her egg, from an admirer, was three feet tall and opened out into two halves. But it's size wasn't the only thing. Inside it contained a cage, exotically decorated with brilliantly-coloured flowers and plants. And darting in and out of the vegetation were two beautiful and gaily plumaged birds — singing merrily, of course!

A girl's husband-to-be must have thought that she had a sweet tooth, he sent her what must have been one of the largest chocolate eggs ever made. Made in Britain, it was ten feet high and contained nearly half a ton of confectionery!

One lovely French actress probably never felt quite the same about eggs again after the one which she received one Easter. It contained a number of scorpions, one of which wound itself round her wrist and stung her. Needless to say, the actress was in hospital for several weeks, only narrowly escaping death . . . and the culprit remained anonymous forever.

Guests at a dinner party in New York were very surprised to find that their host's diningroom was almost filled to its four corners by a giant egg. The remaining space was filled by an idyllic country scene, complete with quacking ducks, grunting pigs, green fields and a babbling brook. But that wasn't all. A gravel path led to a door in the egg, through which the guests found the dining table and feast. But obviously the host wanted to do things properly — he'd decorated the walls of the egg and the table to look just like the white and yolk of a real egg! The guests were egg-static!

them away resolutely. "Crying won't mend matters. I *won't* be missish."

She sat up straighter and suddenly hugged the dog as an idea came to her. Bunch gave a muffled grunt of protest and curled himself up more tightly.

"I know what I'll do! I'll run away, not very far, though. I'll go and hide in the forester's old hut. 'Tis quite deserted now, and I can sleep there, for 'tis a warm summer. Then when the Earl finds I am gone he will be so angry that he will refuse to have me in his London house at all and I'll stay here with Becky." She clapped her hands softly. "Bunch, we are saved."

For the rest of that week Rosalind hugged her plan to herself and was secretly busy with preparations. Becky suspected nothing and by the time the good nurse had found Rosalind's farewell note, telling her not to worry, pinned to the bed-curtains on Thursday morning, the young rebel was already some five miles away in the woods.

Lord Allenstone was purposing to arrive in the village on Friday.

"If he chances to search for me he will think I have gone much further away," Rosalind told Bunch cheerfully over a midday meal of bread and cheese.

Bunch wagged his short stumpy tail and laughed all over his shaggy face but he looked longingly at Rosalind's cloak-bag. Bread and cheese was not much of a meal for a dog, in his opinion.

"Have some more cheese, old man. I could not contrive any meat for you. The butcher would have been suspicious, for Becky always buys from Top Farm."

For the first time Rosalind began to wonder whether she could keep Bunch happily concealed in the woods until the Earl had come and gone. Supposing Lord Allenstone determined to find her and stayed in the village for several days, or weeks, in fact. That idea did not bear thinking about and Rosalind shrugged impatiently although she was uneasy.

"We must save our food, Bunch. We do not know how long it must last," she told the dog. Carefully wrapping the bread in a napkin she packed it into her small bag and set the latter on top of two thick horse-blankets 'borrowed' from the stables,

which were to make a rough bed in the hut. "Now we'll have a walk and what's that?"

Bunch barked sharply as Rosalind straightened up from her packing. A clear, frightened call had sounded through the trees.

"Help! Oh, help!"

"Come on, Bunch."

Picking up her long, full skirts, Rosalind began to run in what she hoped was the right direction. Luckily she trusted more to Bunch's instinct than to her own, and the dog led her straight through the maze of trees and underbrush.

"Where are you?" she paused to call out once, and the answering cry came back, nearer and yet strangely muffled and breathless.

Her short ringlets catching on out-jutting twigs, her blue muslin skirts sadly torn by her passage through bramble and undergrowth, she hurried on after the eager dog.

"Pray hurry, I . . . I'm . . . slipping. . . ." came the muffled voice again after a few moments and, pushing back her hair with an impatient hand, Rosalind fairly sprinted through the tangled greenery. The trees ahead of her were thinning now and with a last hasty dash she arrived on the edge of the wood farthest from her own village.

Abruptly she realised what had happened and felt sick with horror.

On this side the wood was bounded by an old quarry, disused now for many years since an underground river had burst through a deep fissure in the rock and poured through the workings to lose itself some miles away in the sea.

But someone was in the quarry now. Rosalind could see a girl of about her own age clinging halfway down the sloping rockface opposite, only a few feet above the grey rushing water. A gap in the rank grass on the edge above her and a long dusty swathe

downwards showed where she had slipped and slid to her present position.

Panting with mingled fear and haste, Rosalind forced a way through the tall grass and tangle of bushes around the quarry head and finally reached the other side, behind which lay a wide bare heath. Once there, she knelt down and peered anxiously at the white face some twenty feet below.

"C-can you hold on while I fetch help? I w-would not be very long."

"I . . . I doubt it," the other girl said candidly. "My hands are growing numb. Have I far to fall?"

Rosalind flushed hotly. Suddenly the other girl's calm courage made her feel ashamed of her own panic.

"You are *not* to fall," she said firmly. "I'm coming to hold you."

Without giving herself any time to think about it she cautiously swung herself over the edge and began to feel for hand and foot holds.

"Stay there, Bunch. Bark, old fellow *bark*!"

Bunch obediently waited unhappily on the edge of the quarry, giving short urgent barks which grew louder and sharper as he watched his slim mistress slowly climbing away from him. Feeling her way carefully and wishing her long skirts would not get in her way so often, Rosalind went slowly downwards. Once or twice she slipped a little, and there was one agonising moment when an outjutting spur on which her foot rested broke away with a jerk and fell into the river below. Biting her lips to stop herself crying in fright, Rosalind pressed closer to the rockface, trembling with shock. Only the thought of the girl in greater danger below made her move again when the trembling had stopped.

"Now, can you reach my hand?" Crouching on a narrow ledge at last, Rosalind stretched downwards and caught at the other girl's sleeve. "Hold tightly, I'll pull you up."

"Do grip the rock or we shall both go," gasped the stranger, twisting sideways until she could hold Rosalind's hand firmly. "How long . . . how long can you hold me?"

"For a long time," Rosalind panted with more briskness than she felt, "but I am persuaded it would be excessively tedious. Instead, I am going to pull you up here to me. This ledge will bear us both until help comes. Pray don't argue," she added as the other girl looked doubtful. "Now, as I pull, do try to climb up."

It was a grim struggle, but five minutes later both girls crouched, sobbing in relief, on the narrow ledge.

"Though how we are to climb up from here is more than I know," Rosalind said with a gulp, wiping her eyes with the back of a grimy hand for want of a handkerchief.

She looked at her companion a little shyly. In spite of her bedraggled appearance she was plainly of some consequence. Her long-skirted riding habit was of a most fashionable cut, her small elegant boots of the softest kid, and a slender gold chain and pendant hung around her neck. Rosalind glanced down at her own muslin gown, now torn and dirty, and wished she had been able to wear her own riding habit for running away; but Becky would then have sent a groom with her and so ruined her plans.

"I vow I am so pleased to be safely on this uncomfortable ledge that I could sit here for hours," declared the other girl with a shuddering glance at the waters below.

Then she turned to her rescuer. "I'm excessively sorry to have put you in this fix," she went on ruefully. "It was all my own fault that I fell. I *would* borrow the pony from the inn and come riding without waiting for Max or my groom. I deserved that the grey should stumble in a rabbit-hole and toss me over the edge of the quarry. Alack, Max will give me a tremendous scold and say 'tis my hoydenish ways again. I can never

seem to be prim and missish as my governess desires me.'' Her dark eyes twinkled mischievously. ''What a good thing you are not so, either. You would never have saved my life, else.''

''I haven't done so yet,'' Rosalind said hurriedly. ''We are likely to stay on this ledge for ever if we cannot discover a safe way out of the quarry.''

''There will be search parties out long before dusk,'' the stranger said confidently. ''When the pony returns riderless, Max will raise the entire countryside to find me. He . . . oh, quickly, shout with me; I hear voices.''

Together the two yelled at full pitch of excellent lungs, forgetting their respective nurses' often repeated

maxim that 'no gentlewoman ever raises her voice to shout!' Bunch's barks subsided a few seconds later to whines and whiffles of joy, and a moment afterwards two heads appeared over the quarry top, silhouetted against the sky.

''Bella, you're a plaguey nuisance. I've hunted half the county for you,'' drawled a languid, deep-toned voice from above. ''Be easy, we'll have you up in a moment.''

Rosalind's companion gave a shakey laugh.

''Dear Max! He will give me a tremendous scold for this fix, but he's an angel really. He's my step-brother and my guardian too, you know. Oh good, he has brought ropes. . . .''

An hour later Rosalind prepared to say 'goodbye' to her gay new acquaintance. Bella's tall, distinguished-looking step-brother and two stalwart grooms had made light work of drawing the two girls to safety and had speedily carried them to the nearest coaching inn. Here Bella was sent to bed at once, despite her protests, for she was badly bruised and more shaken than she cared to admit.

''Bed, you imp,'' commanded Max firmly, ''while I escort this young lady to her home. You shall meet again soon, I've no doubt.''

'Indeed, I should hope so,'' said the irrepressible Bella, gay in spite of wincing with every move. ''Until tomorrow then, Rosalind.''

''And now, may I know your direction?'' asked Max politely. ''Your parents must be growing anxious about you by this hour.''

''I . . . have no parents alive, sir,'' Rosalind said cautiously, wondering what to do. Somehow after the excitement of the afternoon the prospect of a lonely night in the forester's hut did not seem quite so inviting.

''But you have a home, I am persuaded?''

''Oh, yes, but . . .'' Under his quizzical gaze she flushed hotly. Then, suddenly defiant, she said boldly, ''I must tell you, sir, that I was purposing to spend the next few days away from home for . . . for personal reasons.'' Instinctively she bent to clutch at Bunch's shaggy coat and the dog whined with pleasure.

''In short, a run-away rescuer, a fugitive, I collect,'' remarked Max calmly. ''May one know the reason

for such desperate measures?''

Unaccountably reassured by his calm manner, Rosalind found herself telling him the full story. He betrayed no surprise whatever and she ventured to remark upon it.

''You, you do not seem deeply shocked, sir.''

A completely charming smile crossed his pleasant face.

''My dear young lady, surely you have seen enough of Bella's activities this afternoon to realise that, as her step-brother, I have grown used to being shocked.''

He fingered his slim quizzing-glass, swinging it slowly before speaking again rather more abruptly. ''Tell me, Rosalind, were you afraid when you saw the only way to save Bella falling into the water?''

Remembering that moment, Rosalind shivered.

''Indeed, sir, I was; excessively so.''

''And yet you climbed down to help her,'' he pointed out.

''I . . . I don't understand you, sir.'' Rosalind's blue eyes were puzzled.

'''Tis this: you did not avoid the danger this afternoon, in which you showed great courage. Yet, it often takes more courage to face changes than to avoid them.''

There was a little silence in the inn parlour. Then Rosalind slowly looked up to meet his calm grey eyes. There was a kindly understanding in his level gaze, she realised.

''You are right, sir. I had not thought it but it *is* a coward's trick to run away. Only,'' her lips quivered, ''only there's Bunch, you see. I couldn't bear to leave him, and I think he would miss me. He's been with me since he was a puppy.''

Bella's step-brother stood up, stretching out a strong slim hand to stroke the dog, who licked it pleasedly.

''I will promise you something, Rosalind. You shall have your dog with you in London. Should your guardian refuse him lodging I will ensure that Bunch stays close to you.'' Cutting short her eager thanks, he put her blue merino pelisse around her shoulders and took up his own cloak. ''Come, child, your nurse will be in spasms with anxiety if you do not return soon.''

''There's his lordship's carriage! My what an elegant look it has; crested panels and such! Better far than that hired chaise you returned in last evening." Becky peeped from behind the cottage curtains next day. "Do wait here, child, while I admit him."

In the tiny parlour Rosalind waited nervously, wishing heartily that she felt braver.

"Bella wasn't a coward yesterday in spite of the danger, and I will not be one now," she told herself firmly. "My guardian cannot be more terrible than Grandpapa was in his rages, and . . . and I shall have Bunch with me."

An exclamation of surprise from Becky in the hallway made her get up hastily from her chair as the parlour door was opened.

"My Lord Allenstone and the Lady Bella Allenstone," announced Becky, smiling broadly.

Rosalind gasped in astonishment even as she sank in a curtsey.

"Dear Rosalind, how startled you look!" Pale of face but vivacious still, Bella limped forward slowly to hug her warmly. "Ouch, I am sore still, but never so delighted in my life. I could not believe it when Max told me *you* were my new cousin. I have been glooming on forever thinking I might not like Max's ward."

Stunned, Rosalind returned the hug cautiously, for fear of Bella's bruises, but she was looking at her tall guardian rather apprehensively.

"Are . . . are you not excessively angry with me, sir?" she asked, distinctly subdued.

"He would have been if you had not returned," Bella said with a chuckle. She slipped a friendly hand in Rosalind's and placed the other on the Earl's arm. "Max, suppose I promise never to go riding again without a groom in attendance and Rosalind agrees not to run away again, and then we can forget it all and start afresh?"

Max, Earl of Allenstone, kept his face grave but his eyes were twinkling.

"If you both keep those promises I may be spared further white hairs," he agreed before solemnly shaking hands on the bargain.

"And now for London," cheered Bella. "I have not lived there since I was a baby, so we shall be new to all the fashionable ways together, Rosalind. Best of all, dear Bunch will be there to guard us from our stern guardian," she added with a wicked twinkle at her step-brother.

Rosalind laughed, suddenly happy and unafraid.

"I think our guardian may need Bunch's protection from us sometimes," she said demurely.

The Earl looked amused.

"Undoubtedly I shall," he said dryly. "Come here, Bunch; we men must keep together."

Silver Starball

The Christmas decorations which you see in the shops are very pretty, but they're very expensive, and sometimes it's nice to make something of your own, like the silver starball shown here. Starballs are very simple to make, and you can make large ones to hang from the ceiling and smaller ones to hang on the tree if you like.

All you'll need is:

a roll of tinfoil

a needle and thread

some glue

a pair of scissors

Using a saucer or a larger round plate, if you want to make a large starball, draw several circles on the foil and then cut them out. Divide each circle into eight equal sections and cut along each line towards the centre, but do not cut completely up to the middle. When you have cut along the lines on every circle, twist each section around a pencil, so that it curls up to a point. Then sew two or three circles together, with light stitches through the centre. Don't pull the stitches too tight or the foil will tear. Glue two of these layers of stars back to back and then arrange the point so that the whole thing looks like a ball of points.

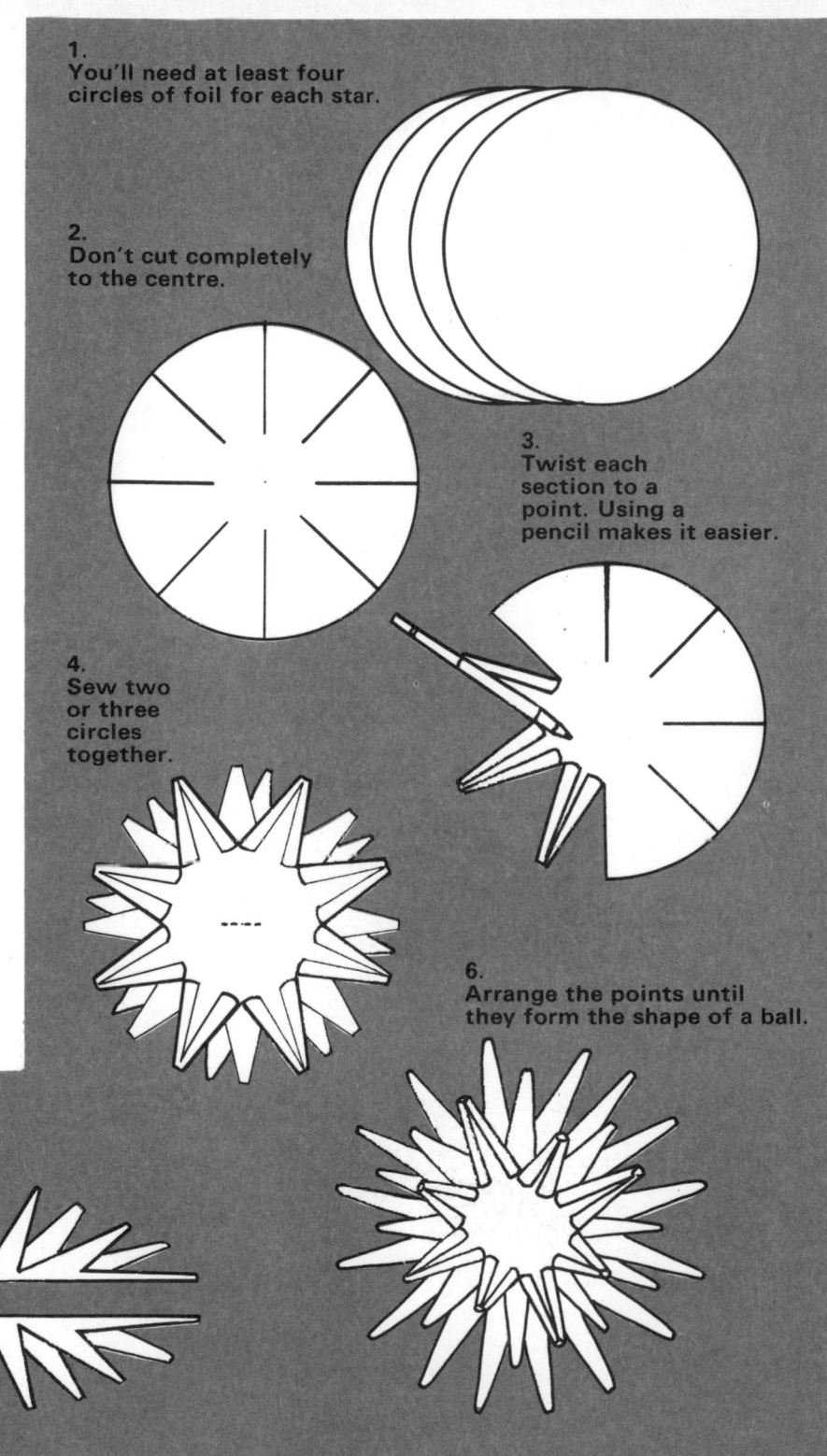

1.
You'll need at least four circles of foil for each star.

2.
Don't cut completely to the centre.

3.
Twist each section to a point. Using a pencil makes it easier.

4.
Sew two or three circles together.

5.
Glue two sewn sets of circles together, back to back.

6.
Arrange the points until they form the shape of a ball.

EYES WITH A

Since its formation in 1934 the Guide Dogs for the Blind Association has brought new hope and confidence to thousands of blind people by giving them new 'eyes' in the form of a specially trained dog which becomes their constant companion. Together this 'unit', as it is called, can travel anywhere they wish . . . to see family or friends, to the shops, to church, or even away on holiday to a strange place.

TRAINING CENTRES

The headquarters of the Association in Britain is at Ealing, near London, and there are training centres at Leamington Spa, Bolton, Exeter and Forfar in Scotland. There are also similar training centres in many parts of the world, including other countries in Europe, South Africa, Australia and the United States of America.

TYPES OF DOGS

Dogs selected for training as guide dogs for the blind are either specially bred for this purpose by the Association or else are specially selected from a litter of puppies when they are a few weeks old.

The puppies which are chosen must have special qualities which will make them ideal for training as guide dogs. The perfect guide dog should be free from nervousness, good-tempered, at home in strange surroundings, and medically fit and free from any illness. When fully grown it should stand 19" at the shoulders in order to maintain the necessary balance between dog and owner.

Some breeds of dog which have these admirable qualities include Lab-

Gypsy patiently awaits further instructions.

COLD NOSE

...confident 'unit' mingle happily with ...shoppers in a busy town.

A helping hand off the bus from his sharp-eyed friend.

...rador and Golden Retrievers, Alsatians, boxers and some collies; but several other kinds of dogs, including poodles, have been used with great success.

PUPPY TRAINING

Once the puppy has had its inoculations, its training can begin at once. This does not take place at the centre, but in the home of an ordinary family . . . probably one just like yours.

Puppies go to selected homes within a radius of thirty miles of one of the centres, and the families who join the Puppy Walking Scheme see that the animal is taught obedience and is taken for regular walks. The puppy is house-trained and gets used to all the noises, such as the telephone and the vacuum cleaner, which go to make up the everyday sound to be heard in a home. It is taught to sit at the curb, and is taught to walk on the left-hand side, in the centre of the pavement.

Although less than half of these puppies eventually become fully-trained guide dogs this is still a much higher percentage among those dogs than among the dogs which are brought in to be trained when fully grown.

A DOG AND ITS OWNER

When the puppy is ten months old it is returned to the centre, where it continues its training for a further five months, this time handled by qualified staff. The dog is taught to halt and sit at curbs, avoid all obstacles which would injure its owner, and cross only when it is safe to do so.

After the dog has passed all these tests satisfactorily, it is time for it to meet its new owner.

This blind person comes to the centre to stay for a month so that he and his 'eyes' may really get to know each other. For the first few days the owner merely gets used to the feel of the harness in his hand, and as he is helped in every way by the staff they also assess his personality so that he can be given the right dog to suit his needs.

Then, together, the newest 'unit' sets off, accompanied by its previous trainer through busy streets, across roads and on public transport. If all goes well the trainer knows that all his months of hard work have been well worth while, and another blind person is on the road to true independence.

When the owner and his dog return home it is on the understanding that he will keep in touch with the centre, sending details once a month of progress, the dog's health and any problems which the two of them might have had to contend with and which might need trained help.

HOW YOU CAN HELP

The Association relies on the generosity of the public to continue its fine work, as it does not receive any aid from the state; and as it costs two hundred and fifty pounds to train a guide dog any contributions, however small, are always gratefully received.

Money can be raised for this worthy cause by collecting milk bottle tops, silver paper and foil. Lots of schools and youth organisations do this and it is surprising how quickly the collection grows . . . but do make sure each piece is clean!

When you have at least two sacks of either foil or silver paper — one sack should be used for each of these commodities as payment for silver paper and foil varies — a letter or telephone call to your nearest centre, if you live within car distance, will quickly bring someone to collect it gratefully.

It not, you can always send it to the following address:

JOHN E. MOORE LTD.
c/o Lewis Foundry Co. Ltd.,
Pencoed Works,
Bynea,
Llanelly,
Carms.

This firm will supply sacks free if no less than six sacks are needed and will reimburse you for the cost of any sack purchased by you under this amount. They will also send you labels which you must mark with your name and address and also state that the contents are for the benefit of the Guide Dogs: e.g. Anytown Grammar School for G.D.B.A. This label must be clearly fixed to the *OUTSIDE* of the sack.

You will have nothing to pay if the sacks are sent by rail. You request the railway to collect from your address and deliver to the address above, which means that you are put to the minimum of trouble. But do advise the buyers first by post so that they will know to expect your material. They will provide postcards for this. Payment is made immediately the consignment is received and checked.

So start collecting now and help to provide more 'eyes with cold noses' for the blind.

HORSEHAIR AND HOOPS ARE IN THIS YEAR

Not this year, of course! But there was a time when all the best-dressed girls were wearing them. Glynis E. Holland reminds us of some fantastic fashions of the past.

For Sale: Parachutes. Highly suitable for all types of underwear, night attire and light summer frocks.

If you saw this advertisement today you'd probably think it was a joke. But thirty years ago the material in an old parachute was too valuable to be wasted.

These were the war years (1939–45), and materials and food were short – so short that they had to be rationed. This hardship made everyone very resourceful, and they found ways of using every scrap of cloth that came their way.

A mattress cover made an ideal winter coat – especially if it was in the ever-popular camel colour. And many favourite handbags were plaited out of such humble fabrics as chair webbing!

THE NECESSITIES OF FASHION

Fashion is dictated by many other things than what the Paris designers have to say on the subject. In the '40s it depended on the available materials, and as these were few the general effect was rather basic, and styles were often austere.

One dress would have to be suitable to wear to school or work in the daytime, to go out in the evenings and to wear again at the weekend. So styles were simple and adaptable. For daytime the dress could be worn plain and unadorned, at the weekends beads and a belt could brighten it up, and in the evenings a lace collar and cuffs might be the special touch to make it different again.

Throughout the centuries and in every country of the world people have worn clothes which were designed to suit their supplies of materials, their way of life, the climate and the mood of the times. And it is surprising how often just a glance at a type of costume can tell us a very great deal about the people who wore it.

Look at a picture of one of the well-to-do ladies of the early 19th century in her elegant Empire line gown and you can imagine her passing her days with a constant round of morning visits, afternoon teas, supper parties and occasional formal dances.

This is the life Jane Austen tells us about in her novels, and even her style of writing reflects the mood of the times. Everything was graceful and unhurried. A lady did not go for long walks alone, would never appear in company with a hair out of place, and usually needed a maid to help her dress.

At this time there was an immense gap between the rich and the poor, and the rich looked all the more elegant in contrast with the shabbily dressed and sometimes starving poor.

Some of the styles and light, flowing fabrics of this period were reminiscent of Ancient Greece. The whole of Greek culture, clothes, architecture, music and way of life was designed to show beauty and harmony.

There was very little difference between men's and women's clothes, and if they wanted to economise they could share the same garment. It has taken us about 2,000 years to get round to a similar idea!

SIMPLICITY AND SHOW

Although the Greeks were rich and luxurious, loved brightly coloured clothes and jewellery – rings on their fingers *and* on their toes – their clothes were always simple and soft.

Compare their loosely draped and flowing tunics and dresses with the elaborate styles and richly decorated gowns which rich people wore in the Renaissance period in Italy. The Renaissance lasted from the 15th to the 16th century, and it means the time when everyone took a new interest in the arts – especially painting. 'Renaissance' means 'rebirth'. You've probably seen this type of painting in art galleries and books – how different it is from the art of the 20th century!

The Italians loved to show off – they built palaces, bought as many expensive clothes as they could afford, and loved acting and their huge paintings.

In the paintings they look very formal, and they stand up very straight. This is because their dresses were so heavy and thick that they could only move very slowly!

They wore luxurious brocades, velvets, satins and silks, and very often they were not content with a plain material and had them richly embroidered. The gowns often had a long train (modern brides preserve this fashion!), and large loose sleeves. Clothes were so expensive that if a Renaissance woman wanted a new outfit she often had to make do with a new pair of sleeves – and so they were only loosely sewn in!

Rich women plaited pearls into

their neat hairstyles and wore diadems encrusted with gems. Younger girls dressed their hair with garlands of flowers.

This description of their make-up might sound familiar to a 20th century reader: they dyed and bleached their hair – blonde was very fashionable – and wore wigs; painted their faces and necks, eyes and lips, and used perfume extravagantly on themselves and – not so familiar these days – on their gloves, shoes and stockings.

WHEN FASHION WAS A BURDEN!

Can you imagine what it would have been like to have been a Renaissance teenager, and not be able to run about because your dress was too heavy!

Or can you imagine yourself in the middle of the 19th century wearing a crinoline so wide that you would need a whole sofa to yourself to sit down on! Your gown would have been made of an enormous amount of material – it might have up to 100 frills or flounces – and about sixty yards of wire would be needed for the hoops!

The word 'crinoline' actually means the material that the supporting skirt was made out of – horsehair (crin) and cotton or linen thread (linum) – and the court of Paris revived the fashion because it was so impressive and, they believed, splendid. We might not agree nowadays!

The huge mass of the skirt was emphasised by the tightly laced waist, a fashion which must have been far from comfortable, and certainly not very healthy.

There was as much controversy about the crinoline, as there has been recently about the mini-skirt. There was a regular battle against it! One of its opponents, Professor Friedrich Theodor Vischer, declared: ". . . the crinoline is an exaggeration which does not add to the beauty of a slim figure, but distorts it . . . And that is surely ugly, very ugly!"

I wonder what the professor would have had to say about mini-skirts, trouser suits and see-through materials.

THE MOOD OF THE '70s

Modern clothes are more casual and less formal than they have ever been before. Girls are accepted in trousers and even jeans, and there is freedom to wear what you want, and what suits you best, rather than what fashion dictates.

This is the mood of the '70s. Everything is very fast moving, and clothes have to be adaptable and comfortable to move around in. Elaborate make-up and hair styles are less and less important – girls are able to be quite natural.

Bright colours have come into our fashion wardrobes – probably because we see them all around us on the huge advertising posters, in full colour films, and even now on colour television.

Nineteen-seventy clothes have variety of styles, of colours and of materials. There has never been so much choice before, and clothes have never before been so comfortable.

So next time you are tempted to complain about your school uniform, think back to the days of the crinoline and the wasp waist, and realise how lucky you are without tightly laced corsets, or huge wire hoops supporting your even larger skirt.

THE FAIRY WIFE

Everyone knows that there are fairies in various parts of the world. Why, in the British Isles, if you cross a certain bridge in the Isle of Man you must, be you peasant or grand royal personage, stop to greet the Little Folk, or woe betide you. Even the Queen of England greeted them, so why should you or I scoff?

I can't tell you the exact place of mystery, but it wasn't *very* far from Caernarvon where the fairies danced beneath the trees or in their fairy rings.

But this particular ring was very bright green, and round it were all sizes of toadstools, suitable for young and old, fat or thin fairy folk, and just *one* extra pretty red-topped toadstool with white dots on it. Nearby was a silver birch covered with catkins and many bushes to shield the dancers from anyone who *might* pass by. . . .

But tonight the fairies decided to leave the shelter of the catkin tree to find a ring in the open meadow.

It was a very risky thing to do, for although humans rarely came that way at all, a late night traveller might well take a short cut across a meadow. Particularly as the moon shone so brightly.

But everyone enjoyed the danger and danced for hours, drinking nectar and eating all manner of fairy cakes. Indeed one little fairy grew so venturesome that she danced to the very edge of the ring – the most dangerous thing a fairy can do!

She was so gay and happy that when she began to sing – why, it sounded as beautiful as a nightingale!

Round and round, here and there she danced like a moonbeam on a lake and when a young man came by and saw her, he fell in love with her that very moment.

He had never, never, *never* seen any one so lovely and because he was a rather selfish young man, thinking only of his own happiness, he ran forward and before any of the fairies had time to say "OH!" he had grabbed her and, in a flash, raced away to his farm cottage in the hills.

A folk story from Wales told by Katherine M. McLean

The poor little fairy shook her head when he told her he loved her.

"Marry me and we will live happily ever after," he begged, when he set her down in the little farm room.

"*Please* let me go," she implored. "Let me go back to my fairy home.

It is not right for humans to wed fairies . . . or for fairies to wed mortals. . . ."

The young man refused to let her go. He told her he would spend his whole life trying to make her happy, but he would not set her free.

The fairy wept bitterly. She knew she was a prisoner . . . so she wept more than ever. But no one can keep on and on weeping, so at last she said: "If you can find out my name I will stay as your servant."

"But I *love* you," he said. "I can't let you stay as my servant."

"I will only stay on those conditions," said the fairy, though she had no idea how to escape.

The young farmer tried every name he could think of and a great many he could *not* think of, which other people suggested, but he *couldn't* get the right name.

He grew more and more miserable. If he didn't discover the name soon he would have to let her go. If she left him it would be as if the sun had stopped shining; if she stayed on as his servant he might, at last, coax her to marry him.

One night as he returned from market, hardly looking where he was going because his thoughts were on the question of the fairy's name, he saw a group of fairy folk near a great bush.

"If I could creep near enough I might hear if they are trying to rescue my fairy," he thought.

Nearby was a ditch which encircled the little wood. He crawled along and dropped into it and, although thorns scratched him and brambles tore at his clothes, he managed to get within hearing distance of the wee folk.

"Why did our sister dance so near to the edge of the ring" wept one fairy.

"Oh, Penelope, Penelope," cried another, "come back to us."

"PENELOPE!" whispered the young man so loudly that he feared they would hear him, but they were so full of their own grief that he was able to get away without detection.

All the way home he repeated the name. How stupid he was not to have thought of it . . . but it wasn't a *Welsh* name and why should a Welsh fairy have anything but a Welsh name?

He pushed open his garden gate, hurried along the path between the two little garden beds, full of flowers, which he had made for the fairy, past the lean-to shed with the house leeks clinging to the old grey slates, like

olive rosettes trimmed with hoar frost.

He flung open the kitchen door and called joyfully: "Penelope, my dearest love, come to me."

The fairy wasn't joyful.

"Who told you?" she asked.

He shook his head. "It's my secret," he told her. "Now you must keep your promise and stay with me –"

"I will keep my promise," she said. "I will stay as your servant."

Nothing he could say would make her change her mind.

Although he would prefer her to be his wife he had to agree or let her go.

How hard the fairy worked.

The little house had never looked so sparkling or fresh; the cows had never given so much milk – such rich milk, too; and the butter was sweet and golden as buttercups. Everyone thought how lucky he was but he knew he would never be content until she married him.

At last she agreed.

" – but," she said, "if ever you strike me with iron you must set me free to go back to fairyland."

"Oh, my little darling," laughed the farmer, "now why should I be striking the most beautiful little lady whom I love so dearly – and with iron, at that?"

"But you must promise," she insisted.

"I promise," he said quickly; thinking what a silly thing it was even to think of! "If ever I hit you with iron you shall be free to leave me."

So they were married.

For a long time all went well.

They had children who were as sweet and dainty as their fairy mother.

Then one day the farmer had to go to Caernarvon Fair to sell a filly. But the animal was so skittish and silly, he couldn't catch her. Round and round; to and fro they careered, but it was no use. The filly pranced and kicked as though laughing at her master.

Losing his patience he called to his fairy wife: "Oh, please, Penelope, come and help me. This filly is leading me such a dance."

Penelope ran to the field and at last they managed to get the filly into a corner. Just as the farmer thought

he had her, she skipped between them and pranced away.

"I'll throw the bridle over her and try to catch her that way," said the farmer when the filly stood still for a moment.

But the bridle missed the animal and hit the little wife.

The moment she felt the cold iron she vanished!

Her husband and children never saw her again.

But often he would tell how once he heard her tapping on the bedroom window pane.

"Look after my little ones," she begged, "please look after them; see they are kept warm and safe from all harm, for I can never return to you."

If ever you meet a person with the surname of PELLING you will know that you are talking to a descendant of Penelope, the little Welsh fairy.

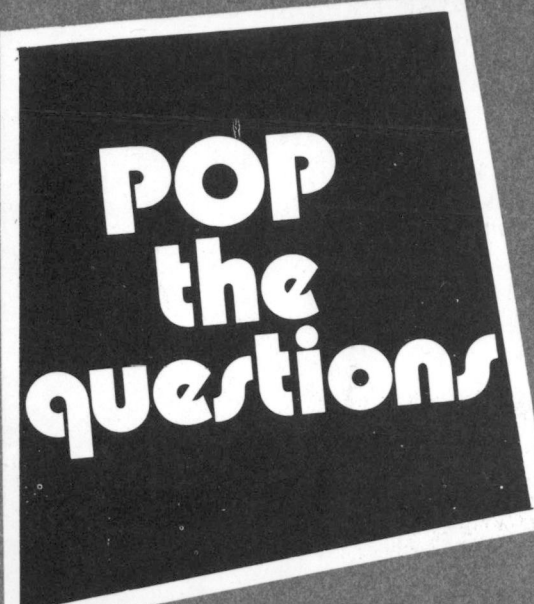

POP the questions

1   A familiar face, drummer of the Rolling Stones. Do you know his name?

2   A true Lady of the Canyon. Who is she?

3   This Mann started his career as a singer and has now turned his hand, successfully, to acting. Do you know who he is?

4   Who is this Highland laddie with the well-known voice?

5   What is the name this singer took from a famous composer?

6   Once in a singing trio, this angel has now made it alone. What is his name?

Answers

1 Charlie Watts
2 Joni Mitchell
3 Paul Jones
4 DJ Stuart Henry
5 Englebert Humperdinck
6 Scott Engel (formerly of the Walker Brothers)